Pen of Flame

CATHERINE BAIRD (1895–1984)

PEN OF FLAME

THE LIFE AND POETRY OF CATHERINE BAIRD

John C. Izzard
with Henry Gariepy

Crest Books
The Salvation Army National Publications
Alexandria, Virginia

copyright ©2002 The Salvation Army

Published by Crest Books, Salvation Army National Headquarters
615 Slaters Lane, Alexandria, Virginia 22314
(703) 299-5558 Fax: (703) 684-5539
http://www.salvationarmyusa.org

Printed in the United States of America

Poems and excerpts from *The Soldier, Reflections, The Evidence of the Unseen* and *The Sword of God and Other Poems* by Catherine Baird are reprinted with kind permission from the publisher, The Salvation Army International Headquarters.

Photos courtesy of The Salvation Army International Heritage Center, London, England and The Salvation Army National Archives, Alexandria, Virginia.

Book and cover design by Laura Ezzell

Library of Congress Catalog Card Number: 2002101930

ISBN: 0-9704870-4-5

CONTENTS

ACKNOWLEDGMENTS

The author expresses his gratitude to a great company of people, too numerous to name, in addition to Salvation Army publications and archival records, who generously shared their remembrances and materials on Catherine Baird.

FOREWORD

John Izzard, long-time friend and admirer of Catherine Baird, has provided a carefully researched and rendered biography of one of the great women of Salvation Army history. He introduces the reader to the pioneer days of the Army in Australia and South Africa and follows Catherine Baird's literary career in the United States and in England. Baird comes alive through historic and humorous anecdotes and through associations with friends, protégés and leaders.

Izzard opens a previously unpublished window revealing facets of the Army's literary history. He shares accounts of the editorial department under siege during the days of the London Blitz. Notable literary personas such as Coutts, Brengle, Watson, Gauntlett, Wiggins and Orsborn move in and out of the narrative. Baird's own quotes give insights to her lifelong ministry with her "pen of flame"—a phrase accorded her by Samuel Logan Brengle, who figures prominently in her life.

When I first met Catherine Baird in 1979, the poet had been retired more than twenty–two years and was eighty–three years old. She was living in the Balham district of London, not far from the International College for Officers in Sydenham where I was appointed as part of the 87th session made up of editors and writers from around the Army world.

Addressing the college of the 87th were many Army luminaries—people whom we knew only by reputation and who were larger than life to us—songwriter Brindley Boon, artist James Moss, the legendary Catherine Bramwell Booth and of course the General, Arnold Brown, and his Chief of the Staff, Commissioner W. Stanley Cottrill.

We were restless with anticipation when we learned that we would meet the renowned Colonel Catherine Baird who had attained the most influential literary post in the Army world and whose songs and poems inspired Salvationists the world over. We claimed her as our own, since she had served several years in the United States where her writing ministry was launched.

I wish I could recall what she said to us on that November day, but I remember only impressions of this figure whose long career climaxed with her distinguished leadership and prodigious literary output at International Headquarters in London. Her tiny frame, unsupported by any cane or walker, spoke a fragile dignity, and the crown of pure white hair seemed fitting, like an angelic accoutrement. When she spoke, her eyes flashed, her voice was steady and strong; her poetic expression and warm, humorous spirit moved us.

It is with pride that National Publications presents this new biography of Catherine Baird to Crest Books readers. It has involved the loving work and cooperation of writers and editors on both sides of the Atlantic. We are indebted to Colonel Henry Gariepy for the skillful abridgement of Izzard's original manuscript which, though too long for this biography, will be available in its entirety in the Army's International and USA National Archives.

Lt. Colonel Marlene Chase
Editor in chief, Salvation Army National Publications
March 2002

PEN OF FLAME

THE CALL OF GOD

Jesus calls from field and city
Through confused and fearful cries
From bewildered, stricken masses
Or a widow's stifled sighs;
Louder than the war–drum's sound,
Soft as tears that stain the ground.

Jesus calls where'er the suffering
Bear their anguish all alone,
Homeless, loveless, lost and fainting,
Needing bread, yet offered stone;
Calls for intellect and will,
Calls for dedicated skill.

Jesus' calls come closer, closer,
From the weary, desolate,
From the friend who stands beside us
Or the stranger at the gate;
Can I fold within my care
Truth He bids me now to share?

Jesus calls, His cross assures me
Of redemption's deepest spring:
Love transforming, multiplying
Whatsoever gifts I bring;
I would in that love abide,
Serving men at Jesus' side.

Jesus, Word of God, I hear Thee
Calling from amid the throng;
I am coming in my weakness,
Fearing not, for Thou art strong;
All things I can do through Thee;
Live Thy life and love through me.

1

A Spark Down Under

On October 12, 1895, when Catherine Elizabeth Cain Baird first looked out at her world in Australia, she made it perfectly clear that she disliked what she saw. Her powers of self–expression, which were to inspire thousands all over the world in her long lifetime, were not immediately appreciated by those who tried to pacify her. Not the least of these was sister Jessie, now eight, to whom Mother had given responsibility for her care.

Ten–year–old Winnie, who had looked after Jessie, Sam and Elsie in turn, looked at Catherine, lying asleep, for once, in the cradle which had been expertly made by her grandfather John Cain. Catherine envisioned the scene later in an article for *The Soldier*:

> Winnie, who had been the first in the family to see Catherine after the doctor left, wanted her more than she had ever wanted anything in her life. She wanted to tell Catherine that the world was, after all, a beautiful place; that there was a grey kitten in a cozy basket at the back of the woodshed. But it was no use. Mother Winifred had firmly said, "No, Winnie, you have Sam and Elsie. The baby shall belong to Jessie and Jessie must care for her when I am busy."

Jessie found her charge of Catherine tiresome, and Catherine seemed to sense this, her angry cry proclaiming that the new baby did not think much of Jessie as a nurse. Winnie, unhappily in the background, longed for the privilege that Jessie clearly didn't want.

"If she's your baby," urged Winnie, "you've got to make her know you love her. Then she won't cry so much." Jessie retorted: "Mother says she never had such a crying child. And I don't see how I can make her know I love her when I don't."

The horrified Winnie, to Jessie's clear relief, there and then offered to take on Catherine just for a while. "Just for a while" continued into the passing days and Catherine responded contentedly. The busy mother was wise enough to turn a blind eye to the "temporary" switch of nurses, as it seemed to be clearly to everybody's advantage, especially Catherine's. A later understanding between the older sisters rendered Winnie's care of Catherine permanent, and thus began the special bonding of the two sisters, eldest and youngest, that was to endure throughout their lifetimes, though they were sometimes separated by thousands of miles.

Catherine Baird's statement in later life that Winnie "practically brought me up" was proven in the early Australian days. When delicate health delayed the start of Catherine's formal schooling, it was Winnie who provided the rudiments of her education. Winnie was never too tired or too busy to explain the meaning of a word. She was never impatient with Catherine, who, book in hand, followed her with questions. Others who offered to help dress Catherine found her plaintively preferring that Winnie should do it.

Winnie persuaded Catherine to ask God to help her think of others. "Do you mean at the penitent form in the Juniors meeting on Sunday?" the little girl asked. "Oh no," said Winnie, "when you know you are wrong you don't wait for any day or place, you kneel down wherever you are. You can ask God now to make you good." She brought out an old wooden chair and, in the center of the kitchen floor, Catherine knelt to pray. For the first time in her life, she felt a need to be forgiven.

Catherine described her oldest sister as "our loving, dependable guide, always like a rock." In her book *The Soldier*, Catherine described Winnie's stabilizing effect on the family in crisis:

> There was a terrible day when the family heard the pronouncement that Mother was going into the hospital, traveling many miles to a distant town. Winnie knew that a great burden was soon to rest upon her childish shoulders for many months; but she never said a word of complaint. In a panic Catherine whispered, "What shall I do if Mother never comes back?" "Nothing," said Winnie firmly; "I'll never leave you; but Mother is coming back." And that was that. But between that day and the day of Mother's return, there were many months of responsibility coupled with hard work when Winnie was both housekeeper and mother.

In her advanced years, Catherine recorded: "My childhood prepared me for the aloneness that could have developed into loneliness. [As] the youngest of our family, I was often alone while my brothers and sisters were at school. Later on, when they were at work and far away from home, I saw them but seldom. As a young Salvation Army officer I was often stationed alone. But with a world full of interesting books and people, how could I be lonely? To be quite honest, I have always needed sometimes to be alone."

Catherine's mother, Winifred Cain, a member of the Anglican Church, was a lover of quiet ways and refinement. Winifred's father, William Baird, slight of build but a strong, often kilted Scot, lived with his grandparents as a boy in Glasgow. As a child, he had known them to be "strict religionists and God–fearing people." William was deeply influenced by them, becoming intensely religious.

At age eighteen, William Baird and a friend had embarked from Glasgow, investing William's small savings in a passage to Australia, where prospects were said to be good. Arriving in Adelaide to work, he first met The Salvation Army and thought them, with their boisterous methods, to be a queer lot of people. He recorded: "However, I was specially impressed by one of them, and in the midst of a great revival I was led to the cross. I was much impressed with the principles of the Army, and felt they were of God."

When William Baird became a Salvationist in May of 1883, the Army was only five years old internationally and not yet three years old in Australia. Later he would be asked to take charge of an Army corps, which led to his acceptance into officership and a vigorous and fruitful ministry in the Army. The sails of Catherine Baird's ultimate destiny were set.

When marching orders came for William to leave his post in Kadina to go to North Adelaide, he reluctantly left there a special young lady for whom he felt "rather partial but who had no time for The Salvation Army." He knew his departure would make a deeper relationship between them unlikely. Nevertheless, orders were to be obeyed, regardless of his feelings. Miss Winifred Cain's attraction to William, however, was not enhanced by his devotion to The Salvation Army. Yet in the immaculate strategy of God, Winifred married William, fulfilling God's plan for their life together.

Catherine's maternal grandparents, John and Winifred Cain, had left the Isle of Man, a pleasant pastoral island off the west coast of England, for Australia. There, it had been rumored, was space and opportunity enough to ensure any willing worker of a happy and healthy existence. Upon arrival, John opened a furniture shop and prospered. His entire family became regular communicants of the Anglican St. Peter's Cathedral in Adelaide.

John Cain took the fourth commandment seriously. After dutifully attending Sunday morning service at the Cathedral with his family, he would spend the remainder of the afternoon at home resting. One day, the visit of a friend, "a godly Scotchman," uprooted John from his sofa for good, at least on Sunday afternoons, by invitation to attend a Salvation Army meeting. John had heard of these strange people and was reluctant. But curiosity prevailed, and John left his Sunday sofa for the Army rally. There he found that these people possessed something that all the forms and ceremonies of his past life failed to bring to his soul. Observing their peace and joy, he longed for the same happy experience and soon made his total commitment to the Lord. His wife Winifred and family followed him into the Army. When the Bishop of Adelaide learned of John's conversion at the Army corps, the kindly dignitary placed his hand on the head of the defecting choir member and blessed him.

The Cains' daughter Winifred was a clever girl. It was her father's pride that she, sitting among the shavings in his workshop, had learned from him to read the Bible at the age of four. Having the benefit of a good education, she became a schoolteacher. Like her father and mother, Winifred had been confirmed in the Anglican communion. She loved the liturgy, and her sense of beauty was satisfied in the silent, lofty church with its long nave, paneled walls and tall candles burning on both sides of the altar.

When schoolteacher Winifred Cain read in a letter from her mother that her entire family had joined The Salvation Army, her reaction was one of deep shock. Reared to love the reverence and ritual of the Church and the culture of its ministers, she found it impossible to fathom how her family could ever identify themselves with what she considered to be a vulgar movement led by ignorant eccentrics.

Reluctantly returning home for summer break, Winifred found that the extent of her family's involvement was painfully obvious. Even their lovely home was an open house for sinners the Army pursued. The last straw came when Winifred found her bedroom taken over by two ladies of disrepute, now converts. Winifred was convinced that her family had gone mad.

Her world was in turmoil. She decided to distance herself from her family and live her own life. But natural ties were strong, and a continual and loving correspondence flowed between her and her sister Katie, who longed that Winnie would make a commitment to Christ and The Salvation Army.

Sadly, it was only when Katie became ill and died that Winifred relented. Too late to soldier together in the Army as Katie would have wished, Winifred knelt in grief beside the coffin of her beloved sister. There and then she foreswore her worldly ambitions and vowed to take Katie's place as a soldier in the Army she had so misjudged.

The way was now cleared for Brother William Baird, then only a private in the ranks, to follow the dictates of his heart. The wedding on December 31, 1884 of Brother Baird and Sister Winifred Cain was one of the first Salvation Army weddings in Australia.

It was a young Army, breaking entirely new ground. Despite severe persecution, The Salvation Army in Adelaide and in many other parts of the Yorke Peninsula continued to grow rapidly. Heavy responsibilities were given to new soldiers with little or no training, who served with dedication and distinction.

There and then began a commitment of far–reaching influence, with William and Catherine Baird serving in two continents. Their children would serve in four.

THE SEERS

Only the lowly and the wise
Hear victory songs in infant cries!
Proud eyes may swiftly turn away
From Jesus' manger bed of hay.
Yet do the pure, with perfect sight,
See chariots of holy light
And heavenly horsemen, clad in power
Invading time each day and hour.
In silent prayer they venture far
Beyond this world's most distant star,
Encounter God in every place,
Where saint and sinner need His grace.

2

In God's Army

Hundreds of Christians in Balham, South London had joined in their traditional procession of witness on the morning of Good Friday, 1984. A very frail Catherine Baird, a colonel in her eighty–ninth year, walked the three–mile route as usual, leaning sometimes on the arm of a friend. Weary she was, but witness she must.

"How did it go?" asked Catherine's friend Sidney Gauntlett afterward.

"Well, people didn't take any notice of us," Catherine replied. "I just had the feeling that I wish they'd pick up bricks and throw them at us!"

The frustrations of the veteran Salvationist and the benign indifference of the Balham populace was a far cry from the experience of Catherine's parents and pioneer Salvationists in Australia's Port Adelaide. Captain and Mrs. William Baird and their colleagues had found no lack of interest from the locals. Even as they had stood in prayer outside their corps hall, a shower of stones fell upon the soldiers. Successive corps appointments followed for the Bairds, each presenting its demands and dangers which they met with the courage and resourcefulness that would be remembered by their daughter Catherine.

The day–to–day financing of a Salvation Army officer's command and his personal expenses were laid unceremoniously on his own shoulders. He was not even guaranteed provision for basic needs of food and clothing. It was an accepted principle that corps expenses had to be met and all bills paid before an officer felt entitled to draw his personal living allowance. Salary was not a right. Like Salvation Army officers the world over, the Baird family was provided a variety of living quarters and made the best of them all, poor or pleasant. At all hours, Winifred Baird could be found seated at her sewing machine, converting donated rolls of material into clothes for the five children.

One day, William Baird took his son Sam to the edge of the cliffs in Newcastle. There, sailing on the Hunter River, was the White Star liner, *Medic*. The *Medic* housed the first Australian soldiers to join the British in South Africa, where war with the Boers raged for nearly two years. The Salvation Army was involved in ministering to the casualties of the conflict, and Sam would always remember its significance. It foreshadowed things to come.

Though taking place so far away, the war in South Africa was an important issue with the Bairds and many others in Australia whose loved ones took great risk for a cause that hardly seemed their concern.

"Why doesn't God stop it all?" a man asked William Baird.

Baird replied, "God has given men the power to choose what they will do. There will always be wars until all men are on God's side. Then they will stop war ... War is a symptom of a disease—like a rash is a symptom of measles."

William Baird's clear opinion of the sickness of war was likely reflected many years later in the convictions of his daughter Catherine, an avowed pacifist.

South Africa, although many miles away, was in reality much closer than the family imagined. Within the space of two short days, two life–changing events occurred.

Seventeen–year–old Winnie Baird, the source of so much inspiration in her little sister Catherine's life, enlisted as a soldier in The Salvation Army, with the full intention of eventually becoming an officer. The morning after Winnie had solemnly signed her name to the Army's "Articles of War," she was in the kitchen with her mother and young Catherine. Winnie answered a loud knock on the door, and brought back a telegram. The mother's hands were deep in a bowl of flour, making the father's special Scotch scones. "You open it, Winnie," she said. Winnie slit the orange–colored envelope, pulled out the message and read: "You are to farewell to South Africa."

In a Mother's Day tribute some time after the death of her mother, Catherine recalled the drama of that moment:

> Father was away on campaign when the cable bringing news of his appointment to a foreign country came to our house. I seem to see her [Mother] now, standing in the kitchen with my eldest sister. They read the

message together. She did not speak but, turning her back to the big colonial fireplace, she lifted her gray eyes and gazed out of the window. No tears dimmed the brightness of her eyes. Yet within three weeks she had left all her kin—father, mother, sister and brothers. She never saw any of them again.

Thankfully, the South African war ended just as the Bairds prepared to travel. The prospect of a journey overseas to a new and exciting country fired the imagination of seven–year–old Catherine.

"We are going to live in a tent in a forest," she announced firmly to her neighbor Julian, "and we shall have tree trunks for chairs and lions for pets."

"You can't play with lions," Julian pointed out, his square boyish face puzzled. "They just eat you when you try," he told her.

"Ours won't be that kind," said Catherine in decided tones. "They'll be glad to have somebody to feed them and look after them. And all our friends will be Black."

Catherine's unalloyed delight at the prospect of leaving Australia for new adventure was not shared by all. Seventy–six years later, in a memorial tribute for Winnie, who was barely seventeen years of age at the time of the Bairds' arrival in Australia, Catherine recalled the anguish involved for her sister, stating the move was "not an easy break for a girl with deep–rooted friendships." She described the backyard bonfire scene when they discarded useless articles as well as old treasured dolls and toys, including Elsie's beloved but delapidated doll. Broken–hearted Elsie clung to her treasure, but as ever, Winnie was there to comfort her little sister and to convince her to be strong. "Close your eyes, Elsie," she said, "and hold tightly to my hand while you part with your doll."

Catherine, excited and preoccupied with the possible adventures in store, was at a loss to understand her mother's rather subdued and wistful air. The pleasures of Africa, she thought, would surely compensate for leaving Australia and their friends and family. But wiser Winnie gently checked her younger sister's insensitivity. "Would you not feel sad if you had to leave us all, without even saying goodbye? That's what mother is having to do."

"How?" asked Catherine.

"The *Persic* does not call at Adelaide," Winnie replied, "so Mother won't see Grandmother and Grandfather, or Uncle Bert and Uncle Jack, not even Auntie Amy."

Since her arrival in Australia, all that was most precious in Winifred Baird's life lay there. The pressures of preparation for the long journey would leave little time for sentimental indulgence, but parting was no less painful and memories were no less poignant. Her mother and father in Adelaide, though so supportive of their officer daughter, would miss Winifred, William and the family immensely.

Even though John Cain and his wife were sad to lose their daughter, son–in–law and five grandchildren to South Africa, the veteran Salvationists were gratified and comforted by the fact that their loved ones were traveling to continue service in the Army. Whether in Australia or South Africa, the cause was the same.

As Winifred Baird prepared to leave Australia and so many who were precious to her, the pain of imminent parting must have been more poignant, for time and travel exigencies, as Winnie had pointed out to young Catherine, were to make impossible even a farewell sight of her parents, brothers and sister. Nevertheless, though rather cruelly denied this comfort, she and the family from then on were to defy the distances which would increase over the years, and kept in close touch.

The September 5, 1903 *War Cry* reported the departure of the Baird family: "At the Melbourne City Temple, the major delivered a farewell address in which affection was expressed for his leader. 'Goodbye, Australia,' he said. 'I am off to do the best I can for God and the Army in South Africa!'"

Catherine recorded the family's last few minutes before they left their lovely home and beautiful garden city of Toowoomba:

> Catherine stopped skipping about, and walked soberly into the bedroom. She found her mother resting quietly, and she stood close to her, tracing with warm fingers the new lines in her mother's forehead. "Are you sad at leaving Toowoomba, Mother?" she asked.
>
> "Yes," said Mrs. Baird, "in a way."
>
> "Why are you going, then?" Catherine asked.
>
> "Because Father is needed in Africa, and a soldier goes where he is needed."
>
> "The lions will be nice to have, won't they?" said Catherine, comfortingly.
>
> "Oh, wonderful!" said Mother, and looking at Winnie, she laughed quite gaily, just as the sound of horses' hooves was heard at the gate and Father called from the veranda steps, "It's time to go!" An hour later the train steamed out and the shunting sound of the engine mingled with the voices of Salvation Army soldiers standing on the platform, singing:
>
> > *God be with you 'til we meet again,*
> > *Keep love's banner floating o'er you ...*

10

On a Thursday afternoon, out of Melbourne, the *S.S. Persic* sailed with the Salvation Army family of seven, all because "a soldier goes where he is needed." For seven–year–old Catherine, this intercontinental journey was the first of several she would make throughout her long and active life of consecrated service.

WE'RE IN GOD'S ARMY

We're in God's Army and we fight
    Wherever wrong is found;
A lowly cot or stately home
    May be our battle ground.
We own no man as enemy,
    Sin is our challenged foe;
We follow Jesus, Son of God,
    As to the war we go.

We shall not lose the fight of faith,
    For Jesus is our Lord,
We lay all carnal weapons down
    To take His shining sword.

When our invading forces march,
    In every tongue we sing;
We are of every class and race,
    Yet one in Christ, the King.
Our Master's darkest battlefield,
    Upon a lonely height,
Reveals God's sword to everyone,
    A cross of love and light.

His kingdom cometh not by force
    But by the gentle power
Of righteousness and truth and grace,
    He triumphs every hour.
Sometimes His happy people march
    With banners floating high,
Though often in secluded ways,
    They fight that self may die.

The good fight is the fight of faith,
    Heaven's victories are won
By men unarmed, saved with the mind
    That was in Christ, the Son.
As morning overwhelms the night,
    So truth shall sin o'erthrow,
And love at last shall vanquish hate
    As sunshine melts the snow.

3

DOORWAY TO DESTINY

C ape Town is at the extreme western tip of the great continent of Africa, by the Cape of Good Hope. Spreading from the sea to the base of the majestic Table Mountain, the city is one of the world's most beautiful.

When Catherine, almost eight years old, arrived with her family, Cape Town had become a large port where ships were repaired, refueled and replenished. It was a main gateway of trade for Africa. The Salvation Army's ministry in South Africa began in Cape Town and thrived there throughout the years.

In later years Catherine Baird described in *The Soldier* her family's journey:

On a foggy September morning, 1903, the *Persic*, like a ghost ship, silently sailed into Table Bay. Winnie and Sam, trying to catch a glimpse of the mountains earlier passengers had described, saw only a wall of fog. Hours passed before the mist thinned, the sun seeming to wrestle for supremacy and quietly absorbing the veil that had hung over sea and land. Busy tugs chugged to the side of the ship, and Winnie, holding Catherine's hand at the foot of the ladder, waited till the swirling waters lifted the tug near enough for her to jump in and for a sailor to lift Catherine into her lap.

As the tug chugged its way landward, voices floated out from the pier. Winnie looked at her father and mother and saw their faces pale, but smiling, as they joined in the chorus:

So we'll lift up the banner on high,
The salvation banner of love;
We'll fight beneath its colors 'til we die,
Then go to our home above.

Once landed, the family was precariously loaded onto a two–wheeled, horse–drawn Cape cart, similar to those in Australia. They rode past lovely buildings, including a castle, through a long road with shops and public houses. After passing small terraced houses, they stopped at Number 2 Congregational Terrace to be greeted by a rosy–faced Salvation Army officer who announced that tea awaited them next door.

Only the youngest member of the party thought the arrival fell short of expectations. "There aren't any lions," mourned Catherine. "We might as well have stayed in Australia."

The installation of Major William Baird as divisional officer, led by the territorial commander, was described by the South African *War Cry* as "an important one to the Western division and to The Salvation Army generally in South Africa."

The geography of their new home differed from the one they left in Australia. The girls' white pinafores now hung on a line slung from one wall of a narrow asphalted square to another and the door opened into a dusty lane, exposed to the rumble of cartwheels and raucous voice of the fishmonger. This was a far cry from the spacious Australian yard, fragrant with honeysuckle, the family was accustomed to. Here they exchanged the scent of blossoms for the smell of fish.

Although Catherine was slow in learning to read, at age eight, she could read a senior high school level book with little difficulty. She devoured every book she could lay hands on, and Winnie and Mother saw to it that only good books lay within her reach.

Though Winnie's heart and eyes were joyfully open to the beauty of nature and people, she was not blind to the ugliness which also existed around her and believed something ought to be done. She had seen White sailors reeling from public houses, drunk and cursing. She had also seen Black girls, no older than herself, earning fifteen shillings a week, while sharing single rooms with five others to support their families. A high percentage of the population had tuberculosis and an equally high number suffered from more dreadful diseases.

Winnie felt her only course of fulfillment was to become a Salvation Army officer. Well aware of the great loss her absence would be to her mother and family, she asked, "Mother, do you mind my going? Sam will always help you." Mrs. Baird smiled. "Winnie," she said, "if you did not want to be an officer, it would break my heart. I shall be so proud of you."

Engrossed in their conversation at the table, they didn't realize the devastating effect the discussion was having on young Catherine. Sitting by the fire, she had her nose in a book but was not reading; she was listening. Jessie was a vague presence for her and not especially fond of small sisters. Sam would never let anyone hurt her. Elsie was a playmate, sharing her toys, books and secrets. But Winnie was the light of her life.

Young Catherine was in a state of shock. From afar, every word of the discussion had affected her deeply and painfully. Her fear and insecurity had reached panic proportions, as that which she long feared was about to happen—the unthinkable loss of Winnie.

When Catherine went to bed that evening, Winnie was there to comfort her. She remained sitting on the bed holding Catherine's hand until the fingers relaxed and the sorrowful eyes closed in sleep.

The nine–year–old Catherine was still asleep the next morning when the divisional commander's letter arrived, announcing Winnie's appointment to the District Six corps until it was time for her to enter the training college. At the time, both Catherine and Winnie did not realize the divine strategy they were involved in. Before long, Catherine herself would go as a Salvation Army officer to the same District Six corps and find there a terrible testing. In its darkness and dismay, Catherine would see a point of light that would illuminate the rest of her life.

Later, following her training and commissioning as a Salvation Army officer, Winnie and her husband Walter Clark would be appointed to Pretoria. It was there that something left its enduring impact upon the youthful Catherine.

Before prayers early one Sunday morning at the corps, Catherine read a scroll on the wall which promised "help and spiritual guidance" to any in need at any time. It was signed: "Walter and Winnie Clark, Servants of all for Christ's sake."

Catherine wanted to be a teacher. She did not like the Army's noisy methods; the loud beat of the drum awakened nothing in her. Books were her greatest treasures. The classroom, not the Army hall, was for her the happiest place in the world. But as she stared at the scroll, she wondered if a servant of all, in the Army, may accomplish more than a teacher. Perhaps a servant in the Army was a teacher of truth that, after all, was more important than geography, mathematics, languages or even literature.

As time passed, Catherine came to realize that her desire to serve was a calling from God. She recorded:

> "In order to use God–given talents, we are constrained to develop them through industry and study, the extent of our efforts being the measure of our desire to serve. Some may be moved by the sight of poverty and hunger or disease and sin; others by a deep sense of responsibility for interpreting the Word of God through preaching or teaching, never forgetting that all Christly service, even the giving of a cup of cold water, teaches and preaches that Word."

Young Catherine took her education seriously. School certificates were carefully preserved as she moved from continent to continent. As time went on, Catherine became an expert with the needle and friends cherished her work. This included a beautiful tablecloth, embroidered with wildflowers— an unexpected gift to Heather and John Coutts, who became lifelong friends.

At the Cape Town corps of Wynberg, Catherine took advantage of the cadet program and its training of youth in evangelism, Bible study, leadership, public speaking, community service and spiritual growth. Catherine's certificates—all first class and still in good condition eighty years later—certify that she was accepted as a corps cadet on July 17, 1912 and progressed up to grade six at nineteen years of age. Later, as an officer in the United States, she would lead her own corps cadet brigade. Some of its members became notable leaders who remained in touch with her for many years.

Upon her father's new social appointment, the family went to live in what became one of Catherine's favorite homes, the Driefontein Farm, a social center for alcoholic rehabilitation near Johannesburg. In her series of articles in *The Deliverer* recounting the lighthearted adventures of "Ethelburga" (undoubtedly herself), Catherine was surely referring to her time in Driefontein. In 1940 she wrote:

> My friend Ethelburga is always talking about the time she lived for two years on a farm where there were fourteen cats, five dogs and all kinds of other animals. Judging from the sparkle in her eyes when she mentions them, this farm must have been Ethelburga's idea of heaven. Ethelburga has been known to save the lonely lump of sugar supplied in a restaurant these days for the cheerful horse who gives her a wink as she goes past him in the lunch hour. And even the most long suffering among Ethelburga's friends are getting a bit weary of having to stop in the street while she strokes every dirty dilapidated feline that sits on a step or wall and turns its talkative eyes toward her.

Catherine's adoration of all creatures may have been encouraged by Winnie, who wanted to tell her, a newborn at the time, that there was a gray kitten in a cozy basket at the back of the woodshed, or by her mother, who was delighted that the children could play and have pets in the garden in Toowoomba. Catherine's legendary love of animals certainly had its fulfillment on Driefontein Farm.

Catherine recalled those days at a gathering she addressed in London:

> My mother never lived in a nice house, as she felt she wanted to be among the people with whom they were working. So we children went to live on a farm way out of Johannesburg. It was about a mile from the nearest house. The men on the farm were those who had expressed a desire to be rehabilitated, and my father brought them there. I loved that farm. It was a really beautiful place and I loved the animals. Everything was just right for me.

Besides the cats and dogs mentioned by Ethelburga, this area also accommodated twenty–eight cows, 112 splendid pigs and one bull. Poultry, including prize birds in well–maintained houses and coops, cared for by Mrs. Baird, produced a plentiful egg supply for breeding and domestic use. Produce of maize, potatoes, barley, oats, 500 fruit trees, acres of strawberry beds and a whole acre for carnations, in addition to the indispensable task of bread–baking, were contained in a day's work at the farm.

At Driefontein, life for the officers was hard but heartening, especially when they saw men respond and prosper, even spiritually.

Catherine loved the farm. The happy and perhaps somewhat sheltered days there may have grown all the more ideal, in retrospect, for days of disturbance and hard decisions would lie ahead. For Catherine, Driefontein was a doorway to her destiny.

LOST IN CHRIST

If Jesus calls, "Launch out into the deep!"
Turn thy ship boldly toward the open sea,
Nor hug the coastline of familiar thought,
However dark mysterious distance seems.
When those, preferring safety and untruth,
Mock thy departing from their cherished shore,
Naming thee traitor, alien, have no care:
The winds are God's and, should thy vessel break,
Plunging thee where the deepest waters are,
Be not affrighted: thou art lost in Christ,
And all who search for thee shall find thy God.

4

POINT OF LIGHT

Catherine wrote to Winnie, "Louis is six–foot–two, and handsome. He has brown eyes and light curly hair and mother says he has a virtuous face, and loves him very much. Of course we shan't marry for a long time."

Winnie was puzzled. Certainly the letter lacked the delight one might expect from a loving engagement. One might even suspect a hint of procrastination. Mrs. Baird was hardly reassuring, worriedly writing of Catherine's reluctance even to go out with Louis occasionally, stating, "I don't know how poor, patient Louis must feel."

It was August 4, 1914. Bold headlines in newspapers blazoned the bad news. Great Britain had declared war on Germany. The news had reached Bloemfontein, the capital of the Free State province of South Africa. There and everywhere else in the British Empire, troubled faces bore the tensions of uncertainty and anxiety.

Leaving the crowded railway station, eighteen–year–old Catherine Baird hastily made her way to meet Winnie. In Catherine's case, her worried appearance had nothing to do with the world situation. Her private world was truly troubled. The baby sister, who had so often turned to Winnie for comfort and guidance, was now grown up, but perhaps at this moment was in greater need than ever of her counsel.

Not that Catherine had sought this visit. It was Winnie's idea. Winnie was missing her husband, Walter, whose gift for fundraising had earned this special appointment and long absences from home. He toured far afield on his motorcycle, seeking support for the Army. It would be good for Winnie to have Catherine around, but the real reason for her sister's arrival was that, for some time, Winnie had sensed that all was not well with her young sister—so much so that Winnie had sent her a telegram.

As the weeks passed, although she was typically helpful to Winnie and her two boys, Catherine was clearly unhappy. Often Winnie watched her sitting in the sun. Dreaming or listless? Winnie wondered which. But she said nothing. Every day fat letters addressed in beautiful sweeping handwriting arrived for Catherine. About once a week, Catherine sat with them before her, chewed at the end of her pen and, in the end, wrote only brief notes.

Things came to a head one day when Catherine, noticing an uncharacteristic sadness about Winnie, realized just how much her sister longed for Walter. Winnie was always so happy when she and Walter were together, sharing everything, but so desolate without him. In contrast, Catherine was painfully aware of the futility of her pathetic attempts at communication with Louis. Obviously very much in love with Catherine, Louis could do nothing but express such love in his letters. But Catherine, with such a rare gift for self–expression, had no such deep feelings to express in return.

Trapped by a love she could not return, her agony was even more acute because she had actually agreed to marry Louis. Dismayed, as they talked, at the difference between Winnie's bond with Walter and her own dilemma, Catherine suddenly burst out: "I wish, O how I wish I felt like that! Louis writes pages and pages and I can't bear any of what he says. I pray over the letters every night—pray that God will help me to write a kind letter in reply, and that He will make me love Louis."

"Catherine! If you don't love Louis, why are you engaged to him?"

"He is very handsome and he said he loved me. I think I didn't like to hurt his feelings." Catherine was tense. Her hands were clenching and unclenching. "And Winnie, isn't it a terrible thing to break a promise?"

Winnie said firmly, "Yes, it is. But to spoil the life of someone is far worse."

Catherine had determined to face anything rather than hurt Louis or break a promise. Now Winnie had turned her thoughts in a new direction. To marry Louis and not to love him would be a great sin against him. Whenever Catherine saw a light she acted quickly, and this time would be no exception. "I'll write to him now," she said, "and just say the truth."

"Yes, just say the truth," Winnie said gently, watching her sister walk away as if a great load had fallen from her shoulders.

A point of light shone in Catherine's heart and mind, by which her whole life—and that of Louis—was dramatically re–directed. Many other lives as well would be affected by it. Other "flashes of light," as Catherine called such insights, were to follow when she needed them most.

As the youngest daughter of pioneer officers, born and bred in Salvation Army quarters and living in the atmosphere of Army officer service all of her young life, it was to be expected that the life of an officer would present itself as an option to Catherine.

She shared in Army activities in many circumstances and conditions, in town, country and by the sea. She had seen its many facets, social and corps ministry, and at the farm at Driefontein, she observed firsthand the wonderful end product of the Army's crusade—the saving of men.

It is noteworthy that Catherine's call to officership—to meet a need—came while she was living at Driefontein Farm, and that a song she later wrote, "His Voice," was written for Men's Social Services, of which her father was secretary.

Due to a breakdown in the town of Kimberley, the provincial officer wrote and asked Mrs. Baird if Catherine could come and fill the breech. She could and did, assisting at Kimberley for ten months. Later, she was called to assist in Cape Town's District Six, "a place of indescribable squalor and evil."

In later years, she was explaining to Quest members—young Salvationists interested in the subject of officership—the origin of her song "Beautiful the Call of Jesus":

> We are called for various things, and I was called to be a Salvation Army officer. When I say "called," I never had any mystical experience, but I was called by a deep, settled conviction: "This is the way."
>
> I was supposed not to be very strong, which is rather funny, isn't it, seeing I have lived to this great age of 60. My mother said, "We will soon find out whether it is the will of God for you to go, because the doctor will not pass you if you are not fit." But they were so short of officers in South Africa, I never got the chance to go to the doctor! And so I went, and I have survived!
>
> Along the way there are various things that will make a Salvation Army officer think, "Was I mistaken? Was I really called?" But you see the disciples knew they were called and it wasn't by any mystical experience; it was by Jesus Christ Himself. Then there was this terrible experience of seeing the One that called them crucified. What was it that held them? It was their call. It was Jesus Himself as a person, and what He taught, and what He was. He was the One that called. There would be something wrong with us if we didn't sometimes have a difficult experience along the way.

Beautiful the call of Jesus
Clear and strong in Galilee,
Calling to the heights of service
Men who harvested the sea;
Gladly they obeyed His summons,
Followed whereso'er He trod,
Til with sight transformed by loving
They beheld the face of God.

When the call of Jesus sounded
From the peak of Calvary,
Clouds of fear and bitter anguish
Veiled the glorious mystery;
But the faithful meekly waited,
Bound together by His call,
And when morning dawned they hailed Him
Risen Savior, Lord of all.

Catherine's own ambition was to become a teacher or a nurse. Neither profession seemed suitable, as she was regarded as a rather fragile child. For the same reason, officership would be an uncertain, even unlikely prospect. Yet the fragile child lived to be eighty–eight, serving as an active officer in appointments—many of them taxing—for forty–two years, followed by an active retirement of more than twenty–six years.

Through her varied work as an editor and her enormous contributions to Salvation Army literature, as well as her notable conference–style platform ability, Catherine certainly proved to be a remarkable teacher, with many grateful students throughout the world. In retirement she spent seven years nursing her friend Miss Dorothy Hunt, in whose large South London house Catherine's flat was situated. She also nursed her own brother Sam as need arose. Her two ambitions, teaching and nursing, were fulfilled in her calling as a Salvation Army officer.

It was wartime when Catherine was called from Driefontein Farm to Kimberley. She plunged into the deep end of officership without the time for a medical checkup, other formalities, or even normal training, although one of the territory's training centers was located in Kimberley itself. Catherine seems to have been trained at Kimberley as a corps assistant, perhaps occasionally attending lectures with other cadets as time permitted. This appears to have been the practice at that time.

The South African *War Cry* of October 2, 1915 extended congratulations to "five lassie comrades—budding officers—whose promotions to Cadet–Lieutenant are announced." Included in the announcement was Catherine Baird. It seems these five were resident at the corps centers named, rather than at the Kimberley training college. Catherine, however, was on the doorstep. At the time, her sister Elsie Baird was a captain.

The discovery of diamonds had led to the sudden development of Kimberly, bringing to the city a rush of hopeful prospectors, miners and a significantly increased population. Unsavory pubs, prostitution and attendant evils also emerged. There was delight and despair as fortunes were quickly made or lost. Catherine arrived to find Kimberley a feverishly busy town, full of people whose happiness was dependent on the prospect of finding a share of the treasures underground.

In *The War Cry* of April 1, 1916 the appointment of Cadet–Lieutenant Catherine Baird was announced from Kimberley to Pretoria, the corps to which her sister Winnie and husband Walter had gone five and a half years before. In the October 21 *War Cry* issue of the same year, her promotion to Sub–Lieutenant was gazetted.

The scroll on the wall of the corps in Pretoria, "Servants of all for Christ's sake," had been designed to attract the needy. But in the divine Strategist's plan it had a much further reach. It had captured the imagination of teenage Catherine, planting the seed of a call which gradually germinated and suddenly came to life at Driefontein Farm. Now, by appointment, Lieutenant Catherine would return, herself a "servant of all, for Christ's sake," to the same Pretoria.

The Pretoria appointment lasted several months until orders came for Catherine to return and assist Captain Walters at Kimberley. Shortly afterwards, both Captain Walters and Sub–Lieutenant Baird moved to Cape Town II, where Catherine would remain until almost the end of the year.

Catherine's next appointment, District Six, low on the slopes of Table Mountain, overlooked the harbor. In certain parts of the district, prostitution was rife, creating red–light areas noted for brawls, thieving and diseases, which often abound in poverty–stricken, overcrowded ghettos. It was a traditional Army kind of parish.

District Six proved to be Catherine's Gethsemane. But the devastating effect upon Catherine was not in any way related to the corps comrades. Rather, it arose from her encounter with its inhabitants, even some of those who attended the Sunday meetings. It was her own sense of horror and hatred of the "indescribable squalor and evil" she witnessed among the dense population—her helplessness and uselessness among it—that brought her to a spiritual impasse.

In the darkness of this dilemma came a flash of light—by which Catherine now saw so clearly—that self–righteousness, and not the evil she so abhorred in others, was the ugliest of all sins. "I realized," she said, "that the prostitutes who loved me were nearer to God than I. My attitude was that of the Pharisee as described by Jesus, and I knew I had to get rid of it. Through my horrified reaction, I learned that unless the seed of God's love in me could be nourished until I was fitted to love the unlovable, I would be useless in District Six or anywhere else. This new knowledge was like a point of light ever increasing throughout the years."

Lt. Colonel Lily Sampson, Catherine's editorial colleague and lifelong friend, had a rare insight into the biographical nature of Catherine's poems. Much of these, she implies, "are mirrors of the inner thoughts of the writer, something too deep to explain." Having learned something of Catherine's inner experience in District Six, Lily Sampson sees in Catherine Baird's poem, "Elder Brother," a confession "of her self–reproach during this time and how God spoke to her."

> He is too cold for love to thaw, I said,
> Too evil for her gentleness to win.
> Through pain and suff'ring he must learn to build
> A house according to the plan of God.
> So, I took eye for eye and tooth for tooth,
> And, when his baseness deepened I, with wit
> And strength and courage more than he possessed,
> Struck him to earth—and worked in loneliness.
>
> Sometimes when moonlight, pale upon the hills,
> Brought heaven near, I heard a ghostly call:
> "Where is thy brother?" From the echoing hills
> The insistent question thronged the peaceful night:
> "Where is thy brother? Where—thy brother? Where?"
> And, in my soul a voice still closer spoke:
> "How darest thou in ignorance decry
> The effectual measure thou hast not bestowed:
> Oh, never was thy love's flame fierce to warm,
> Nor pure to cleanse, nor powerful to heal;
> Nor of radiance to overwhelm

The gloom; nor constant to outlast the night.
So, in the foul pool of another's sin,
Thine own pale impotence thou fain wouldst drown."

I dragged my weakness from its covering;
I looked at it; I held it up to heaven;
And shudd'ring at the sight, retraced my steps
To him I had abandoned. He was gone.
God had descended to the lonely pit—
Where elder sons have oft their brothers cast—
Raised him ... without my aid. Oh, loss! My loss!
I found my brother in the moonlit fields
When heaven seemed near. His welcome drew me in
To share his hearth, his fare; for he had built
A dwelling place far lovelier than mine.

In retirement, Catherine recounted in a BBC World Service talk the District Six experience with young Salvationists who might one day share her vocation of Army officership. She contrasted the happiness and beauty of her home at Driefontein Farm with the misery and squalor of slums of the Cape Town II corps:

District Six was picketed during the war so that soldiers could not get in, because there were hundreds of prostitutes. I did not know what a prostitute was in those days, which I am ashamed to say, because that speaks more of ignorance than innocence. They were lining the streets, and where there was not prostitution there was disease, because the people were herded together in small houses, and they were dying of consumption [tuberculosis of the lungs] in those houses where they often lived five to a room.

It is true that in her first encounter with the raw realities of District Six, on learning how the prostitutes plied their trade, Catherine's horror was beyond measure. That any woman could so degrade herself was to her unthinkable. Continuing to share her conflict and crisis with her conference delegates, Catherine recalled:

Our little hall was like an oasis in the desert, and we had some wonderful Salvation Army soldiers, but on Sunday night the hall used to be filled with the most dreadful–looking people. I thought, "Oh, I hate these people. I don't love them at all. What has happened to that wonderful outgoing spirit I was supposed to have? I haven't got it. Not for these! I'm going home. My mother needs me. I was the youngest in the family and it had meant something to her when I left home. She needs me. They don't." Then I

thought, "No, that's not right. I must ask God what is the matter with me."
And I did.

I had a funny little room upstairs. I discovered shortly after I'd been sleeping in the bed for about a week that it was infested with bugs. One of them crawled up my neck one night. I found that there were three mattresses on the bed, and nobody had ever turned them! I knelt down to pray. I did what we should never do. I opened my Bible and just read anything: took it right out of context. But it said: "The place whereon thou standest is holy ground." So I knew I mustn't leave District Six. I knew I had to stay there, and I said to God, "I cannot, unless You do something for me." And He did. It was a point of light.

"I would not like you to think that I was an especially good person, because I was not," she said to her young audience. "I was just like you!" She was, she implied, like the character in Longfellow's poem she had learned at school—the fable of a young man, persistently climbing, bearing "a banner with a strange device. Excelsior!" Despite discouraging warnings and entreaties from an old man and a young maiden, he had climbed, with determination, upward. In the morning light, high above the Alpine village, they had found him dead:

> But from the sky serene and calm,
> A voice fell like a falling star,
> Excelsior! Excelsior!

I am just like that young man, "Excelsior"—climbing! That is what life is like to me and has been since that moment. It was only a point of light, and it was that point of light which changed my life, because I realized that I must love, unconditionally, everybody. Not just good people; not just people around me; not just the people I loved on the farm; not just my brother who was my greatest love, or my sister who practically brought me up; not just them.

I had to love everybody unconditionally, but it had to be God's kind of love. Sometimes you do not feel the same toward some people as you do toward others. Still, neither do I, but you see God's kind of love is a "willing," and it means that you will their highest good. You will never do anything to practice revenge or hatred or do them harm. You will never rejoice if they fall. You will love with God's kind of love. You will [bring about] their highest good.

From that experience in District Six, her "point of light"—she testified to having found the ability to practice the love she so needed and sought—God's kind of love. Though not yet perfected in her, she was always progressing toward God's perfect love.

Her poem "The New Lieutenant" [see end of this chapter] speaks of the one who "came from the sloping fields among the hills [Driefontein Farm]" to the "sorrowing city [District Six]," where she learned that self–righteousness is the ugliest of all sins. It was a lesson she never forgot.

Toward the end of 1917 came farewell orders. She was to leave Cape Town II for Worcester. Although she had come to terms with District Six, the environment and work at Worcester would surely be a congenial contrast.

Worcester lay in a valley surrounded by farms and mountains. It was an ideal setting—especially beautiful when the snow lay on mountaintops in winter. Having completed her term of probation, Catherine was promoted to the rank of captain on her move to Worcester.

In her eighties, Catherine addressed songster leaders in a conference at Sunbury Court, London. She fondly recollected her association with Dutch, German and Black Christians in Worcester:

> The English people there had taken the country from the Dutch. There were lots of Dutch people there. Their sons were all fighting with the English, but nonetheless they were wonderful to me. I remember it used to be disconcerting on a Sunday. There were quite a lot of Germans in the town and they all used to come to The Salvation Army, as their own minister had been interned by the British. They loved to sing and that's why they came. When I got up to give the sermon they all got up and went out! It happened every Sunday. Even so, the people were so wonderful to me, the Black people, the Germans and the Dutch—all so wonderful.

Surviving typewritten notes of Catherine Baird give another brief glimpse of the Army corps at Worcester:

> No band at all. [A] violinist of German extraction faithfully accompanied us in the open air meeting. In this town there were women whose husbands had died at the hands of British soldiers, but whose sons were now in the British Army, dying for a cause in which the parents could not feel any great faith. Many were Germans, and their husbands were in internment camps. The German minister was there too, and his congregation came to the Army, for they knew we were patriots of the kingdom of which there is no frontier. They felt no ill will toward me; and I shall never forget that when my salary was but three shillings and sixpence a week, my dinner was brought in every Sunday by a German woman whose husband had been killed in the Boer War. On Christmas evening, a party of French, German and English with several [Black] comrades formed a party to serenade the villages.

Catherine's leadership at Worcester was halted by the need for her to enter the hospital, ultimately to undergo two surgeries. Readers of the March 29, 1919 *War Cry* read the good news that "Captain Catherine Baird has so far recovered in health that she is able to work again and is appointed to be statistical recorder at the national headquarters." This would provide Catherine a needful stretch of fallow ground.

Writing under a pen name bestowed upon her, Catherine reported in the April 9, 1938 *War Cry*:

> The Great War raged. Mother's only son, Sam, was on the battlefield. Our father lay ill in the hospital. The terrible flu epidemic furiously swept the country. People dropped in the streets. At one time, Mother went into the courtyard and found four men, apparently asleep. When she approached them, she found they were all dead. Nearly every officer on headquarters was ill, and she could not secure help for a time; most of the shelter staff were ill. Mother went around the huge building making beds that drunkards had slept in. She stood at the end of a long queue waiting to buy a pint of the milk that suddenly had become more precious than gold. She encouraged the remaining few of the staff who served in the kitchen, and were on the verge of panic, and helped them to feel someone was at the helm.

Into the midst of this tragic situation a new sorrow stalked. Although Catherine was home on furlough—only a few weeks since hospitalization—she was out of the home when her mother received shocking news by post. Alerted to trouble at home, Catherine quickly returned there. She recalled:

> I found my mother awaiting me at the top of the stairs—just standing there, motionless and white in the lamplight. "Jessie is dead," she said in a colorless voice. Jessie! One of Mother's children—silent. I could not imagine Jessie's animated body subdued, even by death. I wanted to cry out, but the sight of Mother standing, just standing so lonely and motionless, impelled me to open my arms wordlessly. She came toward me, resting quivering, work-scarred hands against my breast, and I held her tiny body while she wept. It was the first time in my life I had seen my mother weep. I do not know how long we stood there, nor what we said, except that finally she whispered: "You are tired; lie down and I will make you a cup of tea." I found her the next morning comforting a poor, stricken derelict.

As her mother had listened in the night for the repeated call: "Come quickly, a man is dying!" no one except Catherine knew that in her dress her mother carried a letter with the news that her second eldest child had died in far–off Texas.

Soon Catherine herself would sail for that same distant land. In August of 1920 she received transfer orders to the United States territorial headquarters in Chicago. Her mother traveled with her, going by way of Southampton, England. In Chicago she worked in the finance department. Although other members of the family were sad to say goodbye in South Africa, Catherine's brother, Sam, was glad to welcome Mother to his home in Chicago. In due course, Mrs. Brigadier Baird would return to South Africa to her husband and other children.

Sam delighted in initiating his young sister to the new way of life in America, which she later referred to as "that incredible country" and "my dear America."

Nevertheless, for Catherine, there would be mixed feelings. She had loved South Africa. With her sisters and brother, she had grown to appreciate its magnificence, its history and many cultures. As a child she had loved to run free, the wind in her hair and the grass soft under her feet. In such open land-scapes, how could one ever become narrow–minded and confined? True, the imaginative seven–year–old, arriving in Cape Town 17 years before, had been disappointed at the absence of the pet lions she had expected to find. But she had discovered that there was nothing docile about the "lions" she later encountered in her path in District Six. Such were much more real and excit-ing than those in her young imagination, and more ferocious even than those lurking in the bush. These may have devoured her, had not a greater power come to her aid and thankfully remained with her.

THE NEW LIEUTENANT

She came from sloping plains among the hills,
Where sun had gilded fields of corn, and in
Her youthful cheeks, still boasted of his wealth.
Now, in the sorrowing city she could hear
The thunderings of sin and see the flash
Of evil strike his victims till they lay
In hideous helplessness wher'er she walked.
So in amaze and terror she passed by
Folding a cloak about her, lest one see
Her priestly dress and call for comfort, warmth.
Her virgin heart was cold with knowledge new
And awful. This foul place was hell now hate,
A wanton wind, her soul's white covering tore,
Blinded her eyes and left her naked, lost.
'Twas then she felt dry lips upon her brow,
An old and tattered garment 'round her thrown.
"Dear child," a harlot spoke, "I love you so!
'Tis not to camouflage my faith in good.
Take these poor rags and hasten to your fields
Of sun–drenched peace. Your gently lowing beasts
Leave me to die; fate owes me nothing else."
Then was there silence longer than the years.
The girl, with tears, received the faded gown.
Pressed young, soft lips upon the fevered ones:
"Here I abide," she vowed; "you recompensed
My hate with love and clothed my nakedness
With all you owned. You're nearer God than I;
For God is love, and loveless innocence
Is like a clean, white platter without food,
To set before the hungry and the sick."
They stood together in the darkening street,
And Love laid fingers on the girl's sad eyes,
'Til she could see in those black lanes, the sun
That spread His golden mantle o'er high hills,
Reach down to clothe the harlot, sending back
His bright reflection from her weary face.

5

PEACE AND A SONG

In 1920, the Windy City of Chicago was caught in the turbulence of Prohibition and its nemesis, Al Capone. The Eighteenth Amendment, banning the production and sale of alcoholic liquor, had taken effect on January 16. America had gone dry. Temperance advocates celebrated the new law, which they felt signaled heaven on earth. Drinking was declared by William Jennings Bryan to be "as dead an issue as slavery." Countless Americans decided otherwise.

A vast criminal business to produce and sell illicit liquor was created by racketeers to meet the continuing demand. Millions of Americans considered Prohibition an insufferable violation of their rights. Drinking saloons that had been closed under the new law were quickly replaced by thousands of speakeasies. In one year it was estimated that in the city of Chicago alone there were 10,000 such illegal drinking places.

The public consumed alcohol and with it funded crime syndicates. Sometimes, as in Chicago, the public even voted the racketeers into political power. Inevitably, Prohibition failed. Nevertheless, it took until 1933 to repeal it.

Catherine Baird's arrival in Chicago in 1920 had coincided with that of Prohibition. Her own exit from the United States in 1934 just followed its demise by a few months. Thus, in her fourteen–year appointment, she only knew America under this law.

Catherine Baird described Henry F. Milans as "the New York editor who drank himself to death, and then at the mercy seat began forty–five years of useful soul winning service among drunkards." In one of Milans' letters to Catherine, dated May 2, 1932, he writes:

I have noticed that *The War Cry* is giving more attention to the Prohibition question, and I am glad of that. It does seem to me that God must often be terribly disappointed in His professed followers in the Church. In the *Literary Digest* poll of the clergymen, only a bare majority were in favor of keeping the Amendment. I would not be a bit surprised if the Church membership showed up very wet in a similar poll. But I do hope that The Salvation Army will be true to itself, its Founder and its God and stand for the Amendment, even if it stands all alone among all religious organizations. Even if it costs the Army something in its collections. God will furnish better money for His work.

The Army's official stance regarding Prohibition was clear. Commander Evangeline Booth spoke before the House of Representatives in 1930, and continued her speeches on Prohibition until 1932. The following is an excerpt:

The Salvation Army in the United States has a force of over 4,500 officers, who spend their whole time in this work. Their experience endows me with peculiar competence to witness to the salutary effect which the banishment of the saloon has had upon myriads throughout our land. The old degradation through drink has practically disappeared. The field officers universally witness to the changed condition. The wine–room seduction, once so frequent, is now a thing of the past. Let us bless the law that has thrown this protection around the path of American womanhood. Children in our day nurseries and kindergartens come to us noticeably better fed, better clothed, healthier, happier and more teachable. They no longer face the day with the added and greater injury of a bleeding back or blackened eye because of the inhumane beating received at the hands of a parent rendered insane through the delirium of strong drink. Representing a movement that, in its attitude toward the drink question, had never known a hesitating moment, I earnestly entreat that no stain of modification or nullification be permitted to tarnish this most righteous and beneficent law. Before all the world the United States has lifted the standard. Never let that standard be lowered or withdrawn.

Described as America's most powerful and formidable gangster, Al Capone arrived in Chicago in 1920 and blasted his way to the top of an organization of 700 men, eventually controlling most of America's bootlegging. Throughout the twenties, Capone's profits from the illicit liquor trade, the protection business, gambling, vice and sundry rackets were enormous. Once a gunfight began outside the Army's headquarters in Chicago, with one of the gangsters shot, and Catherine Baird seeking to help him just before he died.

Catherine was an undoubted asset to the staff at Chicago territorial headquarters as well as to the USA Central territory. Her secretarial experience at South Africa's territorial headquarters, followed by her own corps leadership in that territory, prepared her for work in Chicago's territorial headquarters, where, on October 7, 1920, she was officially appointed. After a time she served in the office of the chief secretary, Colonel Sidney Gauntlett, a man whose character and ability she admired tremendously. Catherine would also grow to love Gauntlett's family, cherishing it as her own through the years. In Chicago, Catherine worked with Elsie Gauntlett, the officer–daughter of the colonel, who was her own age. They were friends for 64 years. As her own large family diminished with time, Catherine's delightful association with the like–minded Gauntletts remained unbroken and strong.

The former fifteen–year–old corps cadet, reported in the South African *War Cry* as having "soloed sweetly" in a meeting, was now a valued member of the Chicago headquarters songster brigade. This group, which was occasionally accompanied by the staff band, was rather spartan, according to a brief reference among Catherine's papers:

> As a member of the headquarters songster brigade, I sometimes traveled with the band in weather as low as nine below zero. We wore two of everything and more than once an instrument froze and the songsters had to do an extra number.

Sharing life with her beloved brother, Sam, was a great joy connected with Catherine's appointment to Chicago territorial headquarters. From childhood, they had been kindred spirits. Sam had emigrated to America where he had felt there was more opportunity for progress, taking a position with the telephone company. In his search for ultimate truth he subscribed to the principles of Christian Science. Nevertheless, being born and bred in The Salvation Army, he was proud of his family's association and his sister's widening influence within it. Catherine's own search for truth and finding it in Jesus gave her an enormous respect for honesty of thought, and she respected and trusted implicitly in her brother's decision.

On June 18, 1923, Ensign Catherine Baird became editor of the territory's edition of *The Young Soldier*, the Army's newspaper for children. This weekly, popular also with adults, incorporated Christian articles, youthful activities, stories and included the weekly Bible lessons used widely in Army Sunday schools. At the time of her farewell, the editor in chief was Staff–Captain Percival L. DeBevoise, who would remain Catherine's lifelong friend.

Catherine pursued academic studies and courses in editing at Northwestern University in 1923 and 1924. She regarded herself as a life–long student. In retirement, she signed a letter to members of The Salvation Army

Students' Fellowship in her corps of Balham, "Your fellow student." In advanced years she was still to be found in university evening classes, even making arrangements for a London University–sponsored study group.

At a conference at Sunbury Court, the elderly Catherine spoke of her student days in Chicago. Her poem "Ask, Seek, Knock" encourages a questioning spirit, as she explained to the young group, mainly in their teens and twenties:

> He bids thee ask; then do not fear
> Thy spirit's questionings;
> The mind that asketh not must surely be
> Dark as a dungeon, locked and windowless.
> As the first stirring of thy soul His answer comes
> And light, as much as thou canst bear,
> Spreadeth about thee.

In her book of meditations, *Evidence of the Unseen*, Catherine admitted her own misgivings and questionings in her constant search for light and truth—found only in Jesus:

> As a student, I remember being on a sea of doubt. I remember the spot in a Chicago street with the elevated trains roaring overhead. I remember the dress, the hat I wore, the bag I carried, even the little red clasp on the bag—all are bound up with the turbulent thoughts in my mind. Though I must face the storm, I was like the disciples in the boat with the Master sleeping, crying, "Carest Thou not that we perish?" I decided to stay where I was until I found a better companion than He. I have never found one. To those who stay in the boat He is able to give more than any can hold. He is able to show us all more truth than most of us can stand.
>
> That is how it was in my experience, and has been all the way. There has been this continual seeking for truth. It is not a miserable thing; it is a happy thing. It is like Jesus said about the flowers of the field; they do not toil, they are not anxious, seeking for this and that, but they are thrown open to God, and they are clothed more beautifully than Solomon. And so the person who opens himself through that door to Jesus Christ. His soul and his whole personality is open to God and God comes in and God continues giving him more light and more light and more light. There will always be more light. More beautiful visions of God. More understanding of how to cope with this life, because this life is not easy for you. It is a lot more difficult than when I was young. It is a great challenge for you to keep the candle of your faith burning when other lights go out.

Throughout her life, Catherine continued on a pilgrimage of discovery and self–enlightenment by committing herself to the discipline of regular study under the direction of experts, so that her work would show the highest standard of her craft.

Her industry and expertise showed results. When Catherine Baird inherited the editorship of *The Young Soldier*, the paper was only an eight–pager, its content was viewed as amateurish, and circulation was 7,000. In two years, aided by capable veterans in the craft and the editor's own indefatigable pen, the circulation rose to 31,000 and *The Young Soldier* was promoted to the ranks of a sixteen–pager. However, when commended, Catherine was quick to say, "It is not I who have achieved this triumph, but the divisional young people's secretaries and the corps officers. It is they whom you should mention, not me."

Catherine soon became involved in Army life outside the doors of headquarters. Perhaps more than anything else, she enjoyed her association with young people. She gladly accepted responsibility as a young people's local officer, serving at different times as singing company leader, corps cadet guardian, Sunbeam leader and at one time taking charge of a primary section. All of this was an ideal field to enrich the heart and mind of the editor.

Young people were her business. They responded to her interest and knew her as their friend and champion, who would prepare them for service. Her teenage experience of corps cadetship in South Africa, where she merited successive first–class certificates, as well as her comparative youth, made her an exceptional role model. Proof of her worthwhile leadership came even fifty–five years later in letters from four of her old corps cadets, including retired officers of note, recalling happy days in Chicago of 1923.

Brengle Institutes, named after Commissioner Samuel Logan Brengle, renowned early–day exponent of holiness, are Salvation Army retreats that provide a few days for meditation on the blessing of holiness. Catherine's former corps cadet, Milton Agnew, with his wife Kath, in retirement, conducted Brengle Institutes in a number of countries. As a retired colonel, he wrote and thanked Catherine for the foundation she helped lay in his early spiritual life. An affectionate note also came from Lt. Colonel Ernest Agnew, ten years into retirement, who told how that early training under her had opened new vistas of spirituality that led him into active ministry.

Had nothing else come of Catherine Baird's transfer to the United States but her acquaintance with Commissioner Samuel Brengle, the appointment would have been well worthwhile. Catherine had heard of Brengle and read his books as a young officer in South Africa. His nine books received phenomenal circulation. More than a half a million copies of *Helps to Holiness* were distributed, and the book had been translated into 11 languages by 1931.

It was inevitable that Brengle's interest not only inspired Catherine, deepening her spiritual life, but also emboldened her, encouraging the development of her native talents. Brengle became her mentor. "The greatest thing he did," said Catherine, "wasn't preaching, teaching, writing, but being."

Brengle carried on a wide correspondence and, acknowledging a letter from Catherine in 1931, wrote to her:

> I have not been able to read your poems carefully yet but have looked over a few of them and I like them very much. I will look them over further and write you later and send them to you. I do hope that they may be published in book form, though I find there is some hesitation about publishing poems because they have ordinarily a rather poor sale. But I believe these might have a large sale—at least, inside Army ranks. God bless you! He has given you a "pen of flame." Write more and yet more and keep all that you write, for it may be of service later. Ever sincerely, your old friend and comrade, S. L. Brengle, Commissioner.

There were others, who, like Brengle, rejoiced in the "pen of flame," wishing for its widest use in the world and encouraging Catherine to publish her poems. A letter from H. Miles read:

> The Salvation Army has but few writers whose work merits the dignity of "the cloth–bound mausoleum." I hope you won't set it down to biased flattery when I tell you that more than one of your offerings has given me real enjoyment. If the book is published, as it should be, I most certainly want a copy.
>
> From week to week I watch your work. Sometimes I am disappointed; but often enough you rise to the heights and I am repaid. There is enough of the good to make a satisfactory book, and I hope you will discard every line, every number which does not reach the high standard of beauty which you so often realize.
>
> May I dare say a word of warning? Stop writing to "beat the deadline." That weekly column must be a strain at times. Write for practice—always for publication—only when the muse is kind. So far as I know you are The Salvation Army's only poet. Now and then, someone will write a bit of verse sentiment enough to tug at the heartstrings; but none of these writers produce with regularity or consistency enough to merit designation as poets. Salvation Army poetry so far produced in book form has been little better than doggerel. At its best your work is of a very high order. Its measures really sing the words which mere prose cannot utter.
>
> For more than a year Mrs. Miles has carried two clippings of your verses in her pocket book. The writer who can produce that which will urge the read-

er to clip and retain quite obviously is turning out worthwhile work. By all means let us have a book of verse; first, because it's good verse, second, because it would be helpful and inspiring and third, as further proof that The Salvation Army really has a few writers who use ink for purposes other than making literary blots and blobs and by all means keep on writing, if for no better reason than that I like your stuff.

One wonders about Catherine's reaction to this remarkable letter, high in sincere praise, appreciation and kindly advice regarding her work, but quite the opposite about most other Army writers. It would certainly seem that praise from Miles was praise indeed!

The young Catherine's innate love of poetry and its resultant song was undoubtedly encouraged by her mother, home and Salvation Army music–making lifestyle. Nothing, however, is quite like the tremendous influence of one magnificent moment which may last a lifetime, when poetry bursts into life, and all senses are brought into play in the rapturous release of one splendid song.

Such an experience marked the beginning of Catherine's exploration into the beautifully expressed thoughts of other like minds. Without a moment's delay—straight from her participation at a concert in the performance of Longfellow's *Excelsior*—she went home to discover more of the mind of the man she called her "first love" among poets.

At the choirmaster's signal, the voices of 100 boys and girls filled the stately auditorium, clothed in music:

> *The shades of night were falling fast,*
> *When through an Alpine village passed*
> *A youth who bore mid snow and ice,*
> *A banner with the strange device—Excelsior!*

Catherine recorded in her diary:

In the drab old South African school assembly hall we had practiced the mechanics of the song until our youthful throats ached, and I do not think any of us appreciated the words of this exquisite ballad. Now, surrounded by the city hall's plush hangings and gold painted walls, everything seemed glorified. As the alto section, of which I was a member, clung to the haunting echo notes, it seemed that for me the gates of Heaven opened, and for one glorious second I was not the white–gowned child with the conventional beribboned braids, but the aspiring youth of Longfellow's song. I believe I caught a glimpse of the glory that beckoned him higher. That night, after the concert, I borrowed my sister's copy of Longfellow and, unknown to the rest of the family, lost myself in beauty, until my tallow candle burned itself out in a pool of melted wax. Because he had opened for me the portals of new sweetness, Longfellow became my "first love" among the poets.

"My favorites, for the most part," she wrote, "are among the earlier bards, and I do not think modern poets are saying anything that the old masters have not said, nor are they saying it in prettier manner." John Masefield, England's twentieth–century Poet Laureate, she felt, would hardly have claimed superiority over Alfred Lord Tennyson, Poet Laureate of Victorian England. John Milton's *Paradise Lost* and Francis Thompson's *Hound of Heaven* she saw as especially comparable, each describing the Deity and His attitude toward wrongdoers. She observed: "Both poems are ingeniously constructed, and if *The Hound of Heaven* lacks the dynamic force of *Paradise Lost*, this lack is more than supplied by its sweetness of appeal."

Catherine describes Shakespeare's insight into human character as "almost uncanny." A poet, surely to be loved by any admirer of poetry, in her opinion, was John Greenleaf Whittier of the United States. A strong denouncer of slavery, Whittier, she noted, "was a living denial that sweetness of disposition belongs to men too good–natured and holy to fight." She further commented: "We cannot forget those poets, especially loved for their remembrance of children—Eugene Field, James Whitcomb Riley and Robert Louis Stevenson who struggled with physical weakness that would have floored less resilient souls. Stevenson had the happy faculty of picking out happiness from among the debris of shattered hopes."

Thus, at 36 years of age, Catherine shared with her American readers the poets she had learned to love. Without doubt she would gather more favorites through the years.

Catherine had sent two poems to International Headquarters in London. For the first she received such a lovely letter that she was encouraged to write again. The negative response when she did so was devastating. "I got this abominable letter," she said. "You could hardly credit that anybody could write such a letter to somebody they did not know. This letter said I showed "ostentatious display of knowledge." Catherine had used the word "vacillating," only because she had used "changeable" elsewhere and wanted a synonym.

"I got this awful letter," she said, "and of course I was young and I just felt terrible." Perhaps, she thought, "I cannot write; perhaps I had better stop. I do not know that I would have gone on writing because I was the sort of person who easily felt I was wrong and they were right, that perhaps it is true.

Perhaps I never ought to write any more." With typical humility and honesty she shared, "I don't think my writing is important. God can do without it, but I cannot do without giving it to God."

Her poems and articles were well accepted and used in the Army's press in America. In 1927–28, her poems appeared randomly, and were published approximately once a month in 1929. During these years she also contributed short monthly articles. In 1931, her poems appeared weekly, occasionally two in some issues. That year saw a regular column headed: "By our own Bard, Catherine Baird." Her contribution to the American Army papers continued for years well beyond her farewell from the United States.

In her dilemma and distress at the London rebuff, Catherine had decided: "I know what I will do. I will write to Commissioner Brengle. So I did, and I got this marvelous letter from him." An excerpt of the commissioner's reply follows:

> My dear troubled little sister: Bless your heart. ... Go right on writing. Cultivate your talent for poetry. Study, muse, dream, meditate. Pray and write and do not be discouraged. Not everything you write will be tiptop, but much of it will bring distinct blessing to hungry souls.
>
> Write on any and every subject that appeals to you, and don't for a moment consider that you are, or may be, living in a fool's paradise. You are not. You are living in the heavenlies. Abide there to write and tell us what you see, hear, and sense and feel.
>
> You write that you would like to know just what is wrong with your writing. I don't know. Indeed I do not think anything is wrong with it, only not all of it is of equal merit. But that is true of every man who ever wrote more than one thing. Not all parts of the Bible are of equal value, though I would not lose a word of it. Just do you cheer up, little sister and with all good cheer continue to write.
>
> God bless and bless you! Sincerely your old friend and comrade, S.L. Brengle. Joshua 1:9 "What thou seest write in a book."

In 1933, forty–seven poems by Catherine Baird were printed in the United States under the simple title *Poems*, obviously with the goodwill of the territorial commander, Commissioner William A. McIntyre, who made the delightful gesture of sending the first book off the press to Catherine's mother, inscribed:

> Mrs. Winifred Baird: I have pleasure in presenting you with the first book off the press containing your daughter Catherine's poems, in recognition of the fact that you are the mother of this unusual little woman, with a great soul

and a wonderful mind, that has dug into thousands of human hearts, and by her poems, planted there seeds of inspiration and blessing. She is loved and admired by her comrades, and we love and honor her mother for her sake. May this little book be a comfort as well as a joy to your heart. God bless you.

"Inspiration and joy have come to me through personally knowing the writer of these poems," wrote Commissioner McIntyre in the book's foreword. The commissioner had been deeply moved, he said, by Catherine's account of the horrific experiences of District Six in Cape Town, of her revulsion and longing to flee from the situation to a more conducive and cultural appointment. "Instead," he wrote, "she had sought the guidance of God. While upon her knees she received the first real spiritual awakening of her life. The miracle wrought upon her nature in District Six opened a well of spiritual inspiration which has since found expression in her pen."

Brengle was overjoyed to learn of the publication of *Poems*, exclaiming: "Thank the Lord that London is outwitted at last. The years have the last word, not the hours, so let you and I live and work for the years and the centuries and not vex ourselves about the verdict of the hours, which is seldom, if ever, final." Later he wrote to her in a letter:

> The poems you sent me are lovely. I had not time nor inclination to read them critically. Indeed, I have no critical training, and I doubt if I have more than an embryo of critical faculty. I read poetry always for the sheer pleasure and blessing I get from it. All you write pleases me. Your ideas and your unusual use of words surprise and charm and lift me. God bless you. Affectionately, Your trusted counselor and friend. S. L. Brengle. Philippians 1:2–6; Psalms 90:12–17.

On another occasion, Brengle wrote with further encouragement, this time dictated from a hospital bed:

> Thank you for your good little letter with the two lovely little poems enclosed. I love them very much. That little poem "Crown of Glory" is a gem and I had to weep as I read it. The longer poem reaches deep depths in my soul. I love those two lines in which you speak of the "loud and everlasting summons of the deep surging ocean that is God," and that last little prayer for the forgiveness of the world is very tender. I wish a copy of it might be sent to President [Theodore] Roosevelt and some of the leaders. I wish you could get it into the hands of all the preachers in Chicago and New York. If you will give me the privilege I will try to send it around to some of them. God bless you. If the literary critics in London don't appreciate your little poems, they bless

me mightily and I just want you to keep on writing them. Ever sincerely and affectionately, your old comrade and friend, S. L. Brengle.

Crown of Glory

We strove together for the prize. Today
His brow is unadorned—or, so they say!
But I see laurels resting there,
More lovely than the crown I wear,
For he has learned to lose with kingly grace,
To triumph though he did not win the race.

When Catherine's book reached Commissioner Brengle on January 5, 1934, his handwritten letter acknowledged it the same day:

Your blessed little book—autographed—came today and crashed right through my Dr.'s orders to avoid both physical and emotional excitement if I did not want my old heart to go into tantrums. Fortunately I was in bed, resting, or I might have had trouble. It's a gem of a book and I treasure it. I'm so sorry it had to be published somewhat clandestinely; but it will come into its own in time, for it will live. Thank you a thousand times for it! And now go on writing, pray, muse, dream, wait patiently before the Lord and write. God bless and bless you, dear little sister, and fill you with joy and gladness and comforts of the Holy Spirit. Affectionately yours, S. L. Brengle.

Catherine Baird edited nearly 600 issues of *The Young Soldier* and wrote tens of thousands of words for her own publication as well as for *The War Cry*. One non–Army reviewer wrote: "By her popular editorship of *The Young Soldier*, her contributions in the American *War Crys*, devotional articles, short stories and the longer serials, the steady flow of her inspirational poetry culminating in her published book of poems in 1933, Catherine Baird became increasingly appreciated by a varied readership."

Brengle no doubt said it best: "They are written with a 'pen of flame'; they are living poems."

In June 1934, Catherine Baird received marching orders to International Headquarters in London and to the literary department from whence had come the critical comments that had so dismayed and discouraged her! Her appointment was that of editor of *The Young Soldier*, which set the standard for its counterparts in all Salvation Army territories. Her friends and colleagues responded with sorrow at the prospect of missing one who had grown so dear to them, and with joy for the honor she had been given.

Her mentor, Brengle, upon receiving the news wrote to her:

England! *The Young Soldier!* Successor to Mildred Duff! Well, ten thousand blessings be upon you. I'm sorry and glad. We need you over here and we shall miss you, and I fear in some—many, many respects it will not be so pleasant for you there as here. But it is in some ways a greater opportunity and a promotion. It is of the Lord. I shall remember you in prayer, and hope to hear from you when you have time. You will find some lovely people over there whom you will love and who will love you. Get acquainted with Brigadier Ruth Tracy. She is a lovely soul, and was for years on the editorial staff. Don't allow your muse to be idle. It may rest awhile to gather strength for higher flight, but not too long must it rest. The Lord go with you and give you peace and joy and be your confidence and strength.

On a hot Sunday evening on July 22, 1934 the seating capacity of the Chicago Number 5 hall was strained to the limit for Catherine's farewell. The territorial commander, Commissioner William McIntyre, led the gathering. He stated, "Her writings in both poetry and prose have been appreciated all around the world. Her spirit is a leaven that is always at work. Her influence at territorial headquarters has been helpful and inspiring."

Adjutant Baird spoke haltingly, and in a low–pitched voice, of her friend-ships among the American comrades, of her heart–loyalty to the land of Stars and Stripes, of her conception of success as God counts success.

Her brother Sam was of course with her. He would miss Catherine enor-mously, but was proud of the recognition she had been given. He accepted the inevitable loss of her close companionship stoically and with pride.

Catherine was on the way to her fourth continent! Of all said and written, in public and private, the last beautiful word came from her co–workers in the editorial department. Their tribute filled a full long page in *The War Cry* of August 11, 1934 signed, "Toilers on Editorial Row." The following is an excerpt:

We're lonesome on Editorial Row. Now we know what Markham means when he wrote of the martyred president, that like the falling of a lordly cedar he left a lonesome place against the sky. That's it—our sky is blank. She filled such a large place in our lives. There was that about her that was warm—like a hearth fire in wintertime—and refreshing, like a woodland breeze in sum-mer. She has left us—and our sky is empty.

We on "the Row" were proud to speak of her as "our" poet. If Adjutant Baird had never studied the technique of poetry, she still would be a poet. For she herself is a poem far more beautiful than any word of her pen. She is a poem in gentleness. There is no vitriol in her nature. She is a poem in meek-ness, a soul utterly lacking in bombast or self–seeking.

To be appointed editor of *The Young Soldier* at International Headquarters is a distinct honor. Adjutant Baird is the first overseas officer to be appointed as editor of the parent of all Salvation Army junior publications. We rejoice with her in this recognition. We wish her the blessing and benediction of loving hearts. Perhaps no words can meet the need of the moment better than her own verse, which she wrote for another:

> *Peace be to thee—and a song*
> *Pure and melodious*
> *Amid the jarring sound of life's discords.*
> *Grace be thine own cooling stream*
> *Where fires burn on arid desert wastes,*
> *Joy shine on thee—lucently,*
> *When the night grows darkly perilous.*
> *Love shelter thee—constantly.*
> *When the tempest of false creed rages,*
> *Secure in the citadel of God's truth*
> *Peace be to thee—and a song.*

Christ Is All

What worth the careful cunning of my weapons,
The pretty prowess of my mind and hand,
If to a sad bewildered world I'm showing
A bloodless Christ, a shapeless spectral Lord
Set on a pedestal of man's conception
And crowned with rich rhetoric's dainty hand?
Though He be swathed in garb of mighty thinking
And crowned with all the wisdom of the years,
If in His form appear no wound prints,
He is not Christ, the Savior of the world.

Far better if my hand be stayed forever,
And my lips sealed, if I should fail to preach
Crucified Jesus, to a world that's dying,
Crucified Jesus, heaven's beloved Son.
From royal heights He came, His long arm reaching
To miry depths where, lost in endless dark,
My sick soul faintly hoping for deliverance
Watched, eager, for the Bright and Morning Star.

Forbid it Lord, that I be found at evening,
Sailing my ships in muddy shallow pools,
Bagatelle vessels with soft sails and silken,
Moving in circles with no port in view.
Seeking to guide them, let me not be stooping
With downcast eyes and ears that do not heed,
Nor hear the loud and everlasting summons
Of that deep surging ocean that is God.
Soundless its depths and boundless are its waters,
Safe on its bosom strong ships venture far
Toward a country eye hath not yet sighted,
Toward a city men have not designed.

6

A POET WENT FORTH
TO TEACH

Catherine, who had worked closely with Colonel Sidney Gauntlett's daughter, Elsie, in Chicago, would now associate with his son, Major Carvosso Gauntlett—she in the editorial department, he in the literary department. Carvosso arrived at International Headquarters in 1927, appointed to the translations bureau, then later to the main body of the literary department.

Although past correspondence existed between them about Catherine's contributions to *The Officers' Review*, of which he was the editor, they were to meet for the first time. They would discover and enjoy a remarkable rapport, due to their strong convictions and dedication to furthering the Army's usefulness and benefit to its people. Catherine's friendship with Carvosso Gauntlett, his wife Mary and their family was to last a lifetime.

Carvosso's son, Caughey Gauntlett, who became Chief of the Staff in 1982, thought his father's close ties with Catherine Baird were largely due to their like–mindedness and seeing eye–to–eye on many issues. He observed:

> My dad was an intense personality, strictly disciplined, an almost absolute idealist, including ultimate pacifism and strict vegetarianism, but with a keen sense of humor and widely read. When he walked to and from our local station, to and from work, his head was invariably in a book, oblivious of other commuters.

Major Carvosso Gauntlett's handwritten welcome note to Catherine Baird was written on the day of her appointment and was released in London:

International Headquarters, July 9, 1934. Dear Adjutant Baird, A couple of days ago I heard a rumor that you were to "come over and help us," though, for some reason or other, the appointment has not been announced until today. I know I need not assure you of a very hearty welcome. After all I have heard of you, and the letters we have exchanged—as well as your much–appreciated contributions to the *OR* [*Officers' Review*] it will be a personal pleasure to meet you. Smoky old London is not Chicago, and I'm afraid you'll feel the difference in many respects. We haven't the American freedom, etc., but you'll find some great souls on this old building! I came here somewhat prejudiced seven years ago, but I've got to love the place. I feel sure your coming will help to internationalize us afresh. I trust your stay at "101" will be supremely profitable and enjoyable to all concerned. God be with you. Au revoir. Cordially, C. Gauntlett.

It had not been long since Catherine, as a poet in Chicago, had licked her London–inflicted wounds, discouraged by the critical letter from the International Headquarters literary personality. Happily, she had been encouraged and reassured by friends in the United States, such as Commissioners Brengle and McIntyre, to publish her own book of poems. Now she was summoned to the very headquarters from whence had come the offending missive, where she would be honored and entrusted with international influence!

There is little doubt that the officer who sent the critical letter knew he was dealing with a writer of considerable merit, and would have known of the regular flow of Catherine's pen in the Army's American press. The intriguing evidence, however, suggests that the International Headquarters officer who had so squashed Catherine by his caustic comments was the same one who had heavily scored Coutts' literary efforts with blue pencil during his first submission to *The Officers' Review* in the 1920s. Coutts is quoted as saying: "I owe much to him for his wounding, if not at all times tender, it was always the faithful wounding of a faithful friend."

Perhaps the young Coutts, who had never enjoyed "American freedom," was more acquainted with the "blue penciller," and was not as vulnerable as Catherine. True, Coutts had smarted under the pruning, but Catherine had been all but mortally wounded. Perhaps she had previously been a little cloistered and cushioned in the more liberal climate of Chicago. Now in London, she was in the right setting and certainly in the right company to be toughened.

In the long run, however, the offending rocket was defused and rendered harmless. The juniors in America had scored a point over London. Catherine's book had appeared in print. The whole story evolves as a classic fairy tale. As surely as the kitchen–bound Cinderella finally went to the ball and became a princess, the back–room editor in Chicago was not only honored by a call to London, but ultimately invited by the General to occupy the highest literary chair in the Army world.

Catherine Baird had been moved from Chicago, city by a lake, to London, city on a river. The Army's International Headquarters had been long established in the heart of the city's business area, on prestigious Queen Victoria Street, situated between the magnificent St. Paul's Cathedral and the banks of the River Thames. Catherine's "new" office was in fact anything but new, but was part of a large old business house acquired by William Booth in 1881.

The literary and editorial staff Catherine met on her arrival was a fascinating group of people that included Carvosso Gauntlett, Alfred J. Gilliard, Ben Blackwell, Madge Unsworth, Arch R. Wiggins, Frederick Coutts, Reg Woods, Bernard Watson, Gerrit Govaars and Clara Becker. They were described as highly intelligent, collectively unique, but essentially individuals in opinion and character. Their camaraderie was enjoyable, enriching and necessary for mental stimulation.

Ronald Thomlinson, in *A Very Private General*, the official biography of General Frederick Coutts, wrote: "There was a restaurant at International Headquarters for those who could afford the prices, but members of the literary and editorial departments adjourned to the 'blue room,' where there were no tablecloths, to eat their snacks. As quickly as possible after lunch, the group mustered on the top floor, in Clara Becker's office, for lively and sometimes noisy discussion." Among this notable group Catherine found enduring friends like Becker.

Russian–born and clever, Becker had renounced the aristocratic lifestyle of her parents. She joined pioneer Salvationists, trained for three months in Finland to become an officer and, in 1917, was appointed to her home city of Petrograd.

Her willingness and ability brought excessive responsibilities and gross overwork. Under the severe rule of the Bolsheviks and their intolerance of any religion, Becker was persecuted and imprisoned, even enduring solitary confinement. Eventually freed with money sewn in her coat lining, she left Russia in a cattle truck, never to return to work in her homeland. Russia became a forbidden country behind an iron curtain.

Fluent in 13 languages, Clara translated, wrote and taught in Finland until she was appointed to the literary department at International Headquarters, a short time before Catherine, where she joined the translation bureau. One can readily appreciate why Catherine valued the comradeship of such a rare spirit. Each called the other "CB."

Clara had known wealth, but poverty did not frighten her. She was a clever money manager and knew the best shops for value. Her tiny home remained almost empty until she could gradually afford to buy furniture. She did her own upholstery and taught Catherine how to do hers. It was from Carvosso Gauntlett, and not from Clara, that Catherine first learned of her friend's multilingual capabilities.

Caughey Gauntlett shares memories of his very early childhood days when the two "CBs" were regular visitors to the Gauntlett family home. "Cath Baird was always different. She was very quiet in her manner and her speech, unlike the hearty Govaars and the very outgoing Becker. But when she spoke, although one had to listen closely as her voice was so soft, what she said was always worth listening to."

Within the editorial and literary group in London, Catherine happily added to her already enviable number of friends whose young families were equally valued. Frederick Coutts, already known to the others, joined International Headquarters the year after Catherine. "Ensign," as he was known, became a backroom boy in 1935 and remained in the department for the next eighteen years. His ability as a Bible student was recognized and, as a result, he was appointed to prepare the *International Company Orders*—Bible–teaching material for the Army's Sunday school worldwide.

Clearly, there must have been collaboration between the editor of *The Young Soldier* and the author of the *International Company Orders*. A Bible story relating to the *Orders* lesson was a longstanding weekly feature in the young people's newspaper. Baird and Coutts were kindred spirits mentally and spiritually. With much to give in the literary sense, a great mutual respect and appreciation developed between them.

Catherine's early years in London must have been busy and demanding, but she still valued the continued, prayerful support of her old counselor and friend, Samuel Brengle, although the exchanges of letters was less frequent. In the meantime, on September 23, 1935, General Evangeline Booth had conferred on Brengle the highest honor a Salvationist may receive from the Army: admission to the Order of the Founder, given rarely and only to those whose distinguished or sacrificial service would have commended itself to William Booth.

By now Brengle's eyesight had deteriorated considerably. He required help with correspondence and found reading impossible. He was still, however, the old buoyant colleague and teased Catherine good–naturedly about her apology for tardiness in writing to him:

> St. Petersburg, November 16, 1935: My dear Adjutant—Just think, you say you have thought so many times of writing to me, and now comes your lovely letter of October 28th, which shows me how much I have missed because you failed to follow–up your thought with action these many times. It's true I have a very wide correspondence, and am now wholly dependent upon others to read to me and to write for me as I dictate, though I do scribble my name in a big, bold hand.
>
> I am in no sense wholly blind, and the specialists say that they don't think that I shall go blind, but they give me but little hope that I shall ever read again, unless I give my eyes prolonged and complete rest, and this isn't the easiest thing to do. I want my Bible and my song book especially, and I dare not look into them, if I would avoid the very distressing eye–strain and probably worse condition of the eyes. But I can still see the King in His beauty, bless Him, and get glimpses of the "land that is afar off." I suspect the veil is very thin that hides the unseen world from us.
>
> Thank you for all the kind things you say about the bestowal of the Order of the Founder upon me by the General. I am so glad that you and so many comrades approve this. I was teetotally surprised. I never dreamed of such a thing. I did not think that I belonged to the class of saintly, sacrificial souls upon whom the Order is bestowed. Everything I have done has been such a service of love that I have never thought of any honor or reward as due to me. My whole thought has been to give and not to get, and my joy has overflowed in the giving and was its own reward. I do, however, deeply appreciate the honor, and no other has ever quite so deeply touched me.
>
> I will remember your request for a dictated article for *The Young Soldier*. I dictate letters easily, but my articles I have always written with my own hand, slowly, painstakingly, feeling for the right word. In attempting to dictate, I am oppressed with the feeling that the one to whom I dictate may get impatient with delay, but I suppose I must overcome this; indeed I must, or the dear Lord must give me some special inspiration to enable me to dictate more rapidly, if I am to continue to produce articles.
>
> Why are you not writing more poems? Are you too busy, or has inspiration failed you? I hope it is not the latter. Until my eyesight failed me, I frequently read your articles in *The Young Soldier* and was blessed by them. God bless and bless you, dear Adjutant, and make you a blessing beyond all you ask or think. (Eph. 3:20) Affectionately, your old friend and comrade. Phil. 1:2–6.

Having lived for so long in the comparative comfort of American accommodations, Catherine noticed a difference in London, particularly in the early years. Her promotion in status and responsibility carried no equal rise in her standard of living quarters. Quite the contrary. In those days, and long afterward, single officers stationed at a headquarters usually had to find their own accommodations. The weekly allowance, unrealistic for city living, made the search most difficult. One was occasionally fortunate enough to inherit an apartment or live–in arrangement with a family.

Yet surprisingly as expected, most singles took it in optimistic stride, and if they miraculously landed lodgings with their own front door, they rejoiced and considered themselves most fortunate. They would then furnish their primitive place by equally miraculous means, for their annual furnishing grant was as unrealistic as the weekly rental allowance.

By the time of her retirement in 1957, Catherine considered herself most comfortable and fortunate in her apartment, furnished through the years by an annual modest furnishing grant and a retirement allowance. Though she was a department head with the rank of full colonel, there was no hint of complaint or any sense of privation in Catherine. In April of 1979, she wrote to her retired friend in Australia, Lt. Colonel Lily Sampson: "Like you, I am so grateful for this Army flat at a reasonable rent."

The Scottish poet Robert Burns wrote, "Oh, wad some pow'r the giftie gie us, To see oursel's as ithers see us." Catherine had this gift in good measure, revealed especially in the adventures of her friend Ethelburga—the writings confirmed by friends to be Catherine's autobiographical reflections.

Ethelburga's philosophy and light–hearted look at life, as featured in *The Deliverer*, were so typical of Catherine. Through Ethelburga, we see and hear of none other than Catherine Baird herself.

The herculean task of finding a flat in London, armed with so little purse–power, gave Catherine's inimitable sense of humor and imagination free reign. In *The Deliverer* of December 1939 she wrote "Ethelburga—In Search of Independence and a Kitchen."

> My friend Ethelburga has been looking for a flat. If you have never looked for a flat in London—and if you don't know Ethelburga—that sounds simple enough. Seeking for a flat, plus London and Ethelburga, is a complicated business. Ethelburga says she is tired of living in a suburban street where rows and rows of houses as alike as mustard–seed stretch north, south, east and west indefinitely. At one time she vowed she would live either in the city or the country; but the lack of the four guineas per week for one room in the city, and the lack of time to travel back and forth from the country forced her to stoop to compromise at least in the matter of a dwelling place.

Ethelburga claims that her wants are few. So, when we set out on our search, she stressed two simplicities; her need for independence and a kitchen "with a stove and a sink, where you can cook."

Why Ethelburga should need independence when she already has little else, puzzles me. And as for a kitchen, well, few people have seen Ethelburga eat a good meal, let alone cook one. But, as Ethelburga says, she has but two needs. What she did not say was that those two needs are so classified and sub–classified, that they are like the "points" in the captain's Sunday morning address—no end to them.

We trampled many miles. Sometimes we did not go in "because the curtains were dirty and you can always tell the kind of people who live behind them."

The perfect flat, for which Ethelburga left a deposit of a week's rent, turned out not to be so perfect when, after clinching the deal, "the managing lady," who had "looked particularly managing," explained her rules. "You have to wash the front steps and keep the hall clean in turn with the others, though you never use the garden; you must not have the wireless on loudly; or keep a dog; and the lady downstairs is very particular. Oh, and there isn't a water heater or a stove. You'll have these put in your own name, of course."

"Ethelburga" forfeited her deposit, glad to escape from "the particular lady downstairs" and that frightfully ostentatious house. The ideal flat was ultimately found. Ethelburga loved the flat and her privacy—particularly the privacy—though you would never know it from the number of people who have been invited to regard it as "home!"

As Catherine made herself comfortable in her newly furnished London apartment, another letter came from Brengle on December 18, 1935. He acknowledged her recent letter, which he said he would not answer, except to thank her for it from the bottom of his heart.

My dear Adjutant—I am herewith enclosing for you a little article entitled "Flee, Flow, Fight." I think maybe it will be suitable for *The Young Soldier*. I am pegging along, spending about every morning dictating and revising letters and a few little articles, and feel that I am not yet ready for the ash heap and the refuse pile. I am having great joy in my soul these days in spite of dim, old eyes; dull, old ears; a cantankerous stomach and a stabbing old heart. Oh, what a comfort it is to be hid with Christ in God; to live in the secret place of the Most High, and under the shadow of the Almighty and be joyously content with the heavenly Father! God bless you, dear Adjutant. With comradely love to yourself and your fellow–editors, I am, ever sincerely, your old friend and comrade, S. L. Brengle, Commissioner.

On May 20, 1936 the brave and buoyant soldier, whose life illustrated his holiness teaching, was promoted to Glory in St. Petersburg, Florida, from whence he had written to Catherine. A great crowd attended his funeral, conducted by Commissioner Alex Damon, in the New York Centennial Memorial Temple, three days afterward. Unable to attend because she was leading a campaign in Switzerland, General Evangeline Booth associated herself with the service by sending a message.

Where his "little sister" Catherine Baird was concerned, Samuel Logan Brengle had inspired and strengthened her, especially when she had wilted under criticism, and encouraged the publication of her first book of poems in 1933. He had seen her appointed to and established in the international scene in London, and had personally enhanced her life and influence. Both he and she appear to have had the ability to make people feel special, as indeed they sincerely regarded them. Both had large hearts open to all. Without doubt, Catherine reciprocated the inspiration and joy she received from her mentor.

On Whit Sunday, an appropriate day, suggested *The War Cry*, to remember the teacher of holiness, a memorial service was led in the Camberwell Citadel, London, by Major Carvosso Gauntlett. Catherine Baird was there to pay a personal tribute. At the conclusion, after Major Gauntlett had, as he put it, "allowed the commissioner himself to speak," by giving a summary of his holiness teaching, four people knelt at the mercy seat.

From South Africa, Catherine's mother had viewed her daughter's progress with pride. Though many miles apart, they remained as close as ever. Despite the natural desire to be near loved ones, Winifred Baird rejoiced that her children were pursuing their careers with dedication and success. Winnie and Walter were officers in South Africa. Sam was in communications in the United States, and Catherine was at International Headquarters. Mrs. Baird would not have wished her family to be anywhere but where their calling and fulfillment lay. To see them happy made long separation bearable, although her thoughts continually and wistfully bridged the miles.

From London, Catherine followed the fortunes of her loved ones, now spread over four continents. The dissipation of family members was felt most intensely when sorrow was borne in loneliness. Poignantly, Catherine recalled the typical courage of her mother, who, after suffering the loss of her husband, worked her own ministry at the corps in South Africa's East London until her own promotion to Glory in 1935.

A lengthy *War Cry* report, headlined "The Passing of a Warrior," adorned by a fine photograph superimposed on the Army flag, described Winifred Baird's funeral and committal services:

> The news having loosened a flood of affectionate memory in all parts of South Africa and beyond, for her name and fame as "a true soldier of Jesus Christ" are almost a tradition among us. Not only is she remembered by the veterans for her earlier service, but she is in the loving regard of many and many a young Salvationist by reason of her fifteen years work as the corps cadet guardian of the East London corps. It will be difficult too, to think of any other *War Cry* correspondent for that corps for long enough to come.

It would seem apparent from whom Catherine inherited her literary talent. With daughter as with mother, this gift was developed by discipline of study, painstaking practice making perfect. Not surprisingly, Mrs. Baird's sister Amy had also been a correspondent, with contributions in Australian *War Crys* as far back as the 1880s.

From her editorial desk, Catherine became the teacher she wished to be in her youth. She had much experience and skill to impart, and many were wise to heed her advice which greatly improved their writing. One person who appreciated Catherine's timely guidance and encouragement is Brigadier Bramwell Darbyshire. As a young lieutenant, Bram Darbyshire had a moving and defining personal experience that fired his imagination. He records:

> It so intrigued me that I recorded the affair and, on impulse, sent it to *The Young Soldier*. Major Baird replied by return of post and in most encouraging terms, asked me to send her further material for her beloved children's paper. That was in 1937, and it began a series of letters and articles over a period of forty years.
>
> Every story I submitted had a ready response, and there would often be some shrewd observation. She was a constructive critic with a keen instinct for possibilities in any youngsters who wanted to write. One observation stayed with me over the years and helped me as my responsibilities for communication increased, both in the printed and spoken word, and I was grateful for her patient tutorials. We shared a word of prayer in her simple quarters. It was the first and last time I saw her, but she encouraged me to develop a skill which has enriched my life immeasurably over the decades, and which has possibly helped others.

Many recall with pleasure Darbyshire's clever invention of "Woodland Citadel" and the characters and adventures of the wood's inhabitants, among them Brigadier Hawk, Sergeant–Major Crow, Band Leader Owl and other species such as Fred Fox, the euphonium player and the Hamster Timbrelists. This series led to the publication of his book *Woodland Citadel* in 1959.

There followed a succession of other *Young Soldier* publications, illustrated by James Moss, until the mid 1970s, after which Brigadier Darbyshire contributed more than 200 articles in *The War Cry*. "Cath gave me self–belief," writes Darbyshire. "I had no academic background and thought, consequently, I could never write. She once said to me, 'Ideas, not words, are the things that really matter, and you seem to have an unlimited supply of these.'"

Today, an editor's den presents a radically different environment from that of Catherine Baird's time. Transformed are the tools and techniques of the trade. Gone are the galley proofs, printed on strips of paper, typeset from copy supplied by the editors, taken to and returned from the printers by messenger. Today, computers, modern technology and the use of desktop publishing software have revolutionized the editing and publishing process. The paste and scissors, used by editors to cut galley proofs to size and paste layout, have given way to digital layout on the computer screen.

Nevertheless, Catherine Baird related a principle of the editor's task that has not been subject to change: "Like writing, layout is a work of art and is governed by rules, the transgression of which means a clumsy and ugly spread. There is, too, a psychology of type, and whether you know it or not, you sometimes read an article that you would not have read unless it had been set in an attractive and easy–to–read type."

The busiest day in the editor's office life, Catherine reckoned, was "press day"—the day when all final proofs were in front of her and the deadline quickly approached. This day ultimately dictated what would be included in an issue, and what would not. To the modern editor, much of the necessary drudgery of Catherine Baird's day would seem quite incredible. Until 1991, press day for *The War Cry* staff involved a very early morning journey from London to Campfield Press, then the Army's own printing works in St. Albans. There, fortified by a toast–and–marmalade breakfast, they joined in the last hectic hours of proofreading and collaboration with the compositors who, until 1977, set out pages painstakingly line by line.

Notwithstanding all the advances and advantages of today's amazing technology, modern editors would recognize Catherine Baird's editorial principles and priorities to be relevant still.

Catherine found the editor's job to be a never–ending one. "In all probability," she observed, "the editor, on her way to the office, has been writing, reading or thinking out an article. By morning mail, the whole world could invade the small office at International Headquarters for the attention of *The Young Soldier* editor. Correspondence would include literary offerings from the experienced and inexperienced. "The Editor's Den, as well as an Army hall," she wrote, "may be a soul–saving center."

After attention to incoming mail, the editing of copy for the next weekly issue would follow. Catherine described the task as assuring that copy for the printers would be without errors, and "it means selecting the best from all that is worthwhile, and where an idea is lost in an obscure or ungrammatical setting, digging it out and lifting it up. A knowledge of the technique of writing makes this task easy."

Catherine Baird valued her contacts with appropriate experts. Constantly in touch with printers, she would also meet regularly with photographers, artists and other professionals. While not personally qualified in their craft, she, as an editor, would need to know enough of their business to make reasonable requests and to secure the highest standard of service from them. She sought to keep up with the times, to understand the phases of life with which the paper should be concerned. If she were to present Christ as the answer to life's problems, she wanted to know what those problems were.

As editor, she kept pace with Salvation Army activities and concerns, and all their ramifications. "Writing for children, for instance," said Catherine, "and preparing a magazine for their perusal is vastly different from writing about children and preparing a paper about them for grown–ups to read. If *The Young Soldier* is criticized by the boys and girls, that criticism carries far more weight with its editor than would a criticism from an adult. So when a gentleman aged sixty writes in, 'For goodness sake leave *Peter of the Primary* out (a favorite with *YS* readers); we're sick of him,' we politely refer him to ten or twenty letters from the children who like that feature better than anything else in the paper. Thus, the editor of a children's paper looks at the world through the eyes of a child. To do this she has to know children. Her path of investigation leads among them, and among all that concerns them in every way."

"To this editor, at least," said Catherine, "there is nothing more joyous than cooperating with the 'sower who went forth to sow,' by doing what she can, through the pen and the printed word, to plant the seeds of the kingdom in a mind that is open because it is young and receptive—because it is still in the making."

Although Catherine had left Australia when she was but seven years of age, The Salvation Army in Australia regarded her with warmth and pride as her reputation and influence grew. She was still an Australian and belonged to them. Her appointment in 1934 from the United States to International Headquarters was recorded with pleasure in the Australian *War Cry*: "To an Australian has fallen the honor of being appointed to the editorship of *The Young Soldier*, issued from International Headquarters in London." Reports of other important events concerning the Australian in London appeared from time to time and her literary efforts were given a place of pride in the Australian Army press.

On May 12, 1937, Salvationists throughout the British Empire joined in celebrations to mark the coronation of their new king. Headed by large photographs of King George VI and Queen Elizabeth, a full–page spread was carried in the Australian *War Cry* of May 8. Centrally placed was a reproduction of the specially commissioned song, "God Bless the King this Day." The lyrics were written by Major Catherine Baird, the melody by Lt. Colonel James A. Hawkins and the arrangement for women's voices by Bandmaster W. A. Gullidge. The music, reported *The War Cry*, had "the suggestion of a trumpet fanfare," with a prayer for God to "bless the king this day, and all the days that lie ahead," for "A king's is such a lonely way ... A king's is such a troubled way ... A king's is such a lofty way ... He on solitary peaks must stand ... Then, God, reach down Thy guiding hand ... From heaven's loftier slopes."

On Coronation Day in Melbourne's city temple, women songsters from territorial headquarters sang Catherine Baird's song, led by Lt. Colonel Hawkins.

In 1934, Evangeline Booth was elected General of The Salvation Army. She came to International Headquarters in November, preceded by Catherine Baird who arrived in August. Evangeline Booth's biographer, Mrs. Brigadier Margaret Troutt, said: "I rate Catherine Baird as one of the Army's saints. I consider her my writing mentor. She asked me, when I was a young officer, to help with *The Young Soldier*. She always encouraged me and cheered me on." While researching for her biography of the General, Mrs. Troutt was greatly aided in an informal interview in London with her "writing mentor," notes of which have been preserved.

Catherine spoke of the occasion when she had lunch with General Evangeline in her home, shortly after the sudden death of the General's private secretary, Lt. Commissioner Richard Griffith. On the occasion of a territorial gathering in Bristol on October 9, 1938, the commissioner collapsed and died during rehearsals of a singing group he supervised, prior to an afternoon civic gathering where General Evangeline was to lecture. The General, who had led a marvelous holiness meeting in the morning, was so shocked and distressed that she felt unable to remain in Bristol that day. She immediately returned to London, accompanied by the then British commissioner, Charles Rich, who presided over the officers' councils as planned. The General, grieved over her secretary's sudden death, felt unable to touch the harp which had remained covered since the commissioner died. She and he had often enjoyed music sessions together—she with her harp, he with his violin.

Another illuminating window of insight was opened by Catherine for Evangeline Booth's biographer:

> I came to England right after the bank closings in America. The Cosmopolitan Bank in Chicago closed and I lost my money, so I came over here with nothing. The weekly salary was extremely small and I had a hard time making ends meet, after America. Evangeline Booth asked me to help her with something very trivial, and the next day she sent me the money to buy an eiderdown [down quilt]. I hadn't said a thing to her; she just thought of it herself. It was so nice and warm. I was so cold when I came to England; I suppose she was, too. Even if the houses have central heat, it is not the same as American central heat.

In the autumn of 1939, General Evangeline Booth, who had led the international Army since 1934, was due to retire. Army leaders from around the world were summoned to Sunbury Court, a mansion in Sunbury on the Thames, as the High Council to elect a new General.

Salvationists would not ordinarily be aware of the anxiety on the part of certain informed and influential officers who feared that the Army was declining in spiritual power. Its great need—the election of a special General of God's choice for the hour—was the burden of their prayers and a concern expressed to the High Council members. The hitherto private letter is proof of the love and loyalty of its signatories, the first of whom was Catherine Baird. Among the others were leaders who would make their own mark in the future. They were Majors William Cooper, Frederick L. Coutts, Frank Fairbank, Alfred J. Gilliard and Lt. Colonel Carvosso Gauntlett.

> Dear Comrade—The signatories to this letter have felt led to send you an assurance that the deep concern in your heart as a member of the High Council with regard to the future leadership of the Army, is shared by a large number of officers, who are with you in your prayers for God's guidance.

The concern in our hearts is deepened by a conviction that the Army must speedily face developments which are menacing its efficiency. We are driven to this conclusion by the apparent:
—Loss of original simplicity in many methods
—Decline of spiritual power
—Grave loss in numerical strength
—Disquieting financial position

These facts call for a frank approach to the rapidly changing conditions among the people for whose salvation the organization was brought into being. We feel that unless steps are taken without delay, it will soon be too late to rescue the Army from the worldliness and disintegration which attack and destroy all Christian bodies which lose their vision and willingness for self–sacrifice.

Our anxiety is increased because, by the nature of Army organization and discipline, there is little we are able to do to remedy the faults that we see. Many of us have striven and are striving to the utmost of our abilities, but the power remains with the leaders and with the power, the responsibility to God and man.

The facing of these issues and the solving of attendant problems will demand so much time, energy and courage from the Army's supreme leader, that he or she will stand in need of all the adventurous support which can be secured within the ranks. We wish to pledge ourselves to the giving of that support and to the following of a leader who, in making his or her own necessary sacrifices, will demand similar steps from others.

We have given our lives to the maintenance of an organization which was founded and built up by holy daring, self–sacrifice and surrender to the will of God. We are deeply anxious that our new international leader, by his or her personal example in simplicity and devotion, and by the courageous facing of facts, will call forth from the Army of today its latent loyalties to Christ, and to the principles of the flag.

There is no necessity to cumber you with evidence of the need for a courageous and continuing policy. You must be aware of a widespread desire, resulting in many quarters in serious unrest of mind, for the facing of urgent problems, for the establishment of rallying points and above all, for a strengthening of that confidence in leadership which was so great a power to the Army in the past.

We have faith that our leaders, fully surrendered to the Holy Spirit and stripped of all considerations but the urgent needs of the hour, will be guided to choose a General who, by the grace of God, and aided by the experience and vision of those who will be called to advise and assist, will make of the Army the dynamic power which it can be, whatever the cost to themselves.

It is our earnest desire that no reference to this letter or its contents should appear in the public press. Will you therefore regard it as strictly confidential.

Catherine Baird and her brother Sam were friends as well as siblings. An intelligent and thoughtful person, Sam chose not to become a Salvation Army officer as an adult, but his search for divine truth earned him Catherine's lifelong respect. While serving at territorial headquarters in Chicago, Catherine lived in Sam's house, and after a long career working for a telephone company, Sam retired and eventually moved to England to live with Catherine until his death in 1970.

Catherine's appointment to the office of the literary secretary at International Headquarters was a bittersweet victory for the young poet who had felt the sting of literary rejection years before. Still, she would make the most of her time there, learning the latest technology, brushing up her skills as an author and editor, challenging and mentoring staff members, and using her humor and grace to transform the youth publication and change the face of Salvation Army literature forever.

Commissioner Samuel Logan Brengle (left) was Catherine's mentor and guide in her life and writing. Brengle gave Catherine the confidence she needed to use her "pen of flame" for God and the Army. Commissioner William A. McIntyre (right) published and wrote the foreword to her first book, *Poems*, exclaiming that "inspiration and joy have come to me through personally knowing the writer of these poems."

(Clockwise from above) Dorothy Hunt, Catherine Baird, Elsie Baird, Sam Baird and John Einarsen outside the apartment on Bushnell Road in Balham. Dorothy Hunt was one of Catherine's dearest friends, and Catherine cared for her in their home until her death in 1969. Catherine enjoys a picnic in London with Dorothy and a friend.

(Left) Catherine at The Salvation Army's International College for Officers in Sydenham, 1979. Even at 83, Catherine made an impression on delegates, composed of Army editors and writers. (Below) Catherine confers with noted Salvation Army composer Ray Steadman–Allen. Countless composers and lyricists would name Catherine as an inspiration and mentor.

Catherine, 89, completes the annual Good Friday March of Witness in London in 1984. Anxious about her health, several of Catherine's friends had encouraged her not to march, but she was positive it would be her last chance to share her witness to the world in such a powerful way. She joined Christians of various traditions outside the Army's Congress Hall, and completed the strenuous three–mile journey, despite the inclement weather.

(Left) In her last years, Catherine was concerned about the legacy she would leave to the world. Her uncertainty, a trait more visible to those who knew her as an unassuming, quiet young officer (above), was tempered by the affection of her friends and neighbors, who assured her that the work she had done and the compassion she had shown throughout her life would leave an indelible impression.

LINES TO A WRITER

When strong men lie divested of their power,
When youth is robbed of beauty's early flower,
When silver tones like echoes slowly die,
And useless riches all corroded lie—
Thy work shall teach the beauty of His will
When thine own heart is cold and thy lips still;
For unto thee, most honored among men,
As to another one, He gave—a pen;
His hidden secrets haloed in new light
To thee He whispers, then He bids thee: "Write!"

7

A Multi-Edged Sword

Catherine Baird could not help but feel the tremors and devastation of war as London and its people suffered greatly. She shared her feelings during this time:

> Although the newspapers forecast war, I found it incredible that mankind had learned nothing from the glaring truth that wars aggravate rather than solve international problems. Yet, coming from my "digs" one morning en route for 101 Queen Victoria Street, I encountered busy workmen digging underground shelters. Outside my office overlooking the Thames, newspaper boys were shouting ominous messages from the headlines.
>
> Just before the blitzkrieg began in earnest I visited friends in Norfolk. I found it inspiring to leave the little house where the radio blared out the woeful tidings, seeking the quiet of the open fields, and finding sustenance for the tragic experiences that lay ahead. The Salvationist, of course, cannot remain among the good news; but he must never forget it.

To help others be aware of the "good news" she composed her reflection on that topic.

> *Good News*
>
> *Come ye yourselves apart ... and rest awhile (Mark 6:31).*
>
> *Come into the open; toss the latest paper down;*
> *O never mind the placards that are stirring up our town,*
> *For here is news—good news!*
> *'Tis not about the atom pile, the riots or the pound,*
> *Nor where, in case of flood or flame, a shelter may be found;*
> *My news—good news!*
>
> *This morning very early, without the slightest sound,*

A blade of grass pressed upward from her hiding underground;
A rosebud shyly opened up a secret treasure chest,
And, shaking out a velvet gown, how silently she dressed!
The warm winds bore her fragrance o'er the meadows by the sea,
And, passing by my window, poured it freely over me.
My news—good news!

O listen to the heartbeats of the sunny summerlands!
A lad has left his horses while beside the sea he stands,
His hands are rough with toiling; his head, as ever, bare,
The friendly winds come frolicking to rumple up his hair;
An ordinary fellow, knowing kinship with the sod,
Yet, this morning, very early, his soul communed with God.
My news—good news!

Lt. Colonel William Burrows, one of the Army's literati, described Catherine as "a sweet, gentle person. Along with Frederick Coutts and Ben Blackwell, she was a devotee of her 'boss,' editor in chief, Carvosso Gauntlett, and like them, an avowed pacifist, even in the midst of the Second World War." Indeed, from its outbreak, Catherine Baird had already taken a pacifist stance with the above–named, along with Reg Woods and Bernard Watson in the literary department.

Ron Thomlinson, in his biography of General Coutts, writes of those in the editorial department: "They were convinced that for believers to take up arms was inconsistent with the Christian faith. No one had the right to kill another human being, but pacifists were not so much tolerated as despised. Their views were thought to be synonymous with cowardice and disloyalty. In that respect certain members of the editorial and literary departments became 'notorious' for their well–stated views."

Nevertheless, most felt that meeting force by greater force was the only immediate answer to the threat of an evil and advancing enemy. Catherine confessed, "I formed the opinion that it was wrong to disregard the bravery of those who were fighting for freedom." Catherine, at peace with God, herself and the whole world, had the courage of her own convictions. In general, pacifism was not associated with The Salvation Army. Thomlinson adds: "Of course not everyone in the editorial department shared these views, and that gave rise to tension within the work situation."

The armies of Nazi Germany had invaded defenseless Poland. In a final attempt to stave off a war which had increasingly threatened Europe, the British government issued an ultimatum to Adolph Hitler. Receiving no response, Britain declared war with Germany on September 3, 1939—a conflict that would develop into world proportions and last for six years.

No one remained unaffected by the catastrophe, and no age group was exempt from its consequences. In an amazing exodus, city children were evacuated to safer country districts and even to the British dominions. Military reservists were summoned and conscription of Britain's able–bodied young men and women proceeded. Women in the thousands joined in munitions assembly and agricultural work. Volunteers hastened to join civil defense organizations. Human and material resources were confiscated for use in the war effort—even to the removal of metal railings surrounding gardens, homes and other premises, which were to be recycled into weaponry. Food was rationed, gas masks were to be carried by all.

The Army's *War Cry* speedily moved from London to a house in St. Albans. Somewhat unwillingly, *The Young Soldier* followed, but soon returned to the capital. The brief transition, as it affected its editor, was recorded by Ethelburga in *The Deliverer* of December 1939:

> Next morning, Ethelburga heard that her firm was evacuating, and she was instructed to pack up and depart for the country at once! She departed, armed with a suitcase and memories of the perfect flat to which she did not know when, if ever, she would return. As an evacuee, she economized drastically to keep the rent of the flat paid; food being the easiest to go without.

In the gloom of the enforced blackout, millions of Britons apprehensively awaited the inevitable death–dealing invasion by enemy aircraft. "We will raze their cities to the ground," Hitler boasted on September 4, 1940. The Nazis bombed London, cities and villages, factories and fields. It was not until March 29, 1945 that the last bomb fell on British soil. The ferocity of the air raids exceeded preconceived fears. But the courage and fortitude of all under the terror that rained upon them, night after night, was almost unbelievable.

As Chicago's Editorial Row had suggested in their farewell tribute, Catherine Baird's slight frame was no indication of a frail spirit or constitution. Her performance in the blitz proved that although tiny, Catherine was tough. Corps sergeant major Desmond R. Rix remembers a visit by Catherine Baird to Letchworth corps in the North London division:

> In September 1940, at the height of the London blitz, [she] conducted a young people's harvest weekend at Letchworth. At the close of the Sunday evening meeting, the air raid sirens having already sounded, it was apparent

from aerial activity and a glow in the sky, indicating fire over London, that a major attack was taking place in the capital. Corps officers and local officers tried to prevail on the major to stay the night and return on Monday morning. She graciously declined, insisting that it was her duty to return by train through the raid to her home in Balham in order to be at the office first thing on Monday to "put her paper to bed."

"I will tell you about the glorified hole," Catherine recorded in *The Salvationist Reciter* in 1950.

Unglorified, it came into existence one dark night [October 14, 1940] almost as soon as the raid warning had sounded. Scarcely had the sirens' moan died away that the heavy drone of planes flying low was heard. A moment of ominous quiet preceded the shriek of bombs, streaking through the darkness to find their mark.

That evening, the divisional commander Major Edgar Grinsted and his wife had remained on guard at the divisional office, a stone's throw from the scene of the bombing. She had slept under the desk on the floor; he had prepared to snatch what sleep he could in an old chair, too weary for fear.

Suddenly, the crash—the silence—then the sound of running feet and hurrying ambulances speeding. High–explosive bombs had pierced the surface and plunged into the tube railway station, where scores of people were gathered for shelter. They were trapped now under the collapsed roadway, with masonry and huge concrete slabs at drunken angles on them and around them. Water and gas from broken pipes gushed in.

Anybody but the most courageous and undaunted of rescue parties would have felt such a situation to be hopeless. Each man who went down to do his life–saving task did so at the risk of his own life, and so awful were the conditions there that the workmen needed to change over at given intervals. Yet the voice that came over the telephone at the divisional commander's office was quite cheery; could the Army mobile canteen come and serve tea or anything hot to the workers? The Army could and would.

All gas and light were cut off. But the major, back from working in other shelters and traveling with the mobile canteens, called for help to light fires, and soon the canteen and its driver and attendants were off. They found men with grimy faces, wet clothing and haunted but courageous eyes. Quietly and without panic, those who were not killed or trapped were piloted out and taken to hospitals and other shelters. Shrapnel fell all around the Army canteen while its attendants served hot tea in the unsheltered street; they were too busy now to know either fatigue or fear.

They could see the outside of the hole—nearly half a street long and filled with shops and tram–lines and pieces of road. A London bus lay among the debris. Down deep in the hole the station master sat in his office at the telephone, speaking to his headquarters, reporting the incident in slow, measured tones, so that no mistake on his part, nor misunderstanding on theirs, could bring about further tragedies on the line. While he talked the water crept over his feet and up and up. But he still spoke steadily. Then the water folded cold arms around him. This voice faded out. The station master was no more. He was a Salvationist.

In those last moments before the flow of water was halted, a mother drew an old shawl closer round her baby son. She knew she was trapped between the cement slabs. The call of the rescuers sounded faint. She had forgotten her own body. The baby was her world. Cold and menacing, the water crept upward to her waist. She raised the baby and pressed his [hair] against her face. Then she could feel the heavy wetness pressing against her breasts. She raised him again. The water was rising slowly now, but certainly. She jerked her head up; she could hardly feel the baby's body. Her arms were high over her head and almost numb. So she remained for two hours.

Later, when ministering to the people, a fair–haired officer heard her story. Almost timid and quite ordinary in appearance, she explained why "he" was so precious. She did not know that she had glorified a ghastly night.

Afterward I passed the hole every day. Within a few weeks, most of the shops that had not been bombed had been reopened and were "carrying on." Long before daylight and after dark, workmen were busy. All along the side of the road their materials—cranes, great stone cylinders, iron rafters and intricate tools—made gigantic outlines in the dimness. The repairing that once had seemed impossible began to appear possible. The men whistled as they worked. In the spring, they said, the work of reconstruction would be complete. And they kept their word.

Spring has come—many times since, and although long queues of shoppers stand where the hole once yawned, the grass is lush and green on the commons and the tender leaf buds are shyly showing themselves to eyes that have waited for them through chilly, grey months.

When I now walk homeward over the covered hole, I remember the station master at the telephone 'til death claimed him, the uplifted arms of the young mother, the friendliness of the Salvationists—and I know the once–yawning gap has been wrapped about with the eternal fabric of love and courage, friendliness and joy.

In the midst of the rubble and ruin, an incredible buoyancy and sense of humor surfaced and became legendary. This was greatly appreciated by Catherine, who wrote in the USA Central territory's *War Cry* "London Letter," of December 14, 1940:

I feel very humble in the presence of the spirit of London. I see proved, before my eyes, the truth that violence cannot destroy spirit. It can batter and hurt the dwelling and all that surrounds it, yet when force has done its worst it has but given a setting out of which fineness of character shines the more brilliantly.

For one thing, you can't separate the Londoner from his humor. Every new day brings us fresh sights of shopkeepers carrying on as usual, amid the ruins of former places of business which have taken a lifetime to build. An almost demolished barber shop bore this sign: "We have had a close shave; what about you?" Another man had written on a post outside his shop: "Hitler was our last customer; will you be the next?" Finding his plate–glass window smashed one morning, a shopkeeper wrote in black, large letters on a white board: "More open than usual."

With dogged perseverance every Londoner, as soon as one way closes, is finding another way of carrying on.

Catherine, high in praise of others, would not be expected to "blow her own trumpet" but Lt. Colonel Lily Sampson, an established writer retired in Australia, sounds it for her. In a tribute to Catherine, acknowledging the unsung heroes of the London blitz who "persevered day after day, week after shattering week, for years amid the bombings," Sampson wrote:

> Of these, Catherine Baird was one, who often walked to work, sometimes taking over two hours, climbing over and around broken brick and stonework, fire hoses, rescue vehicles, workmen toiling at ghastly craters with cranes and trucks.

In another of her "London Letters to America," in December 1940, Catherine relates events when she accompanied the divisional commander, Major Edgar Grinsted, and his wife to serve refreshments in one of the largest underground stations in London:

> Two hours before the night–raid warning sounded, the Salvationists were at their posts with huge urns of tea, piles of sandwiches, pies and cake. When the raid began, the people no longer came to us, so we descended the emergency stair to them.
>
> As the night wore on, they settled down to sleep on the hard floor, huddled generally so as to allow as many as possible to have room. Most of them had only blankets, or maybe a small cushion. There were little babies, and I noticed that nearly all of them had been bathed and put into clean clothing. We slept beside our people. We huddled together and shared one blanket between four. We had wanted to know how it felt to spend the night like this.
>
> They would accept nothing free. Some of them wanted to pay more than the small price charged for tea [two cents a cup] and sandwiches. Their attitude was one of gratitude for the subway sleeping place, rather than of complaining about the circumstances that necessitated their being there.

"You going to be here in the morning?" they asked, casually. But the look of relief that followed our answering "yes" showed that the question had been far from casual.

At 4:45 A.M. we got up and tried to make ourselves a little bit neater. Our uniforms were old. We were glad, for this was no place for "smartness." We wound our hair up with more speed than skill, and we were glad our Army bonnets covered its disarray. We felt more like crude but useful vessels than dainty ornaments, you may be sure. I stood and looked upon the still sleeping crowd. Relaxed and unconscious, they looked weary in the pale light. But I knew that in the morning they would hide all this behind humor and gruff happiness. I shall never enter a tube station again without feeling that it is permeated with the courage of these folk.

In the chilly dark, we took our places behind the urns [that] the driver of the mobile canteen had left at the exit. We worked by candlelight, for the blackout laws are rigidly enforced now. The morning was black, and rain poured down steadily. Outside, trams trundled along, guns thundered, shells cracked, shrapnel fell—and we served with hearts into which a new quality seemed to have entered overnight.

The "all–clear" signal had not yet sounded, but the stream of persons moving out into the shining darkness seemed endless. The divisional commander was standing behind me, watching their white, cheerful faces and still twinkling eyes. They all [even little children] carried great bundles of bedding. Some were taking bottles of hot tea with them, for their homes were no more. I was conscious of a new understanding of why "God so loved the world." The human race is worth loving.

"You going to be here tonight?" a voice called out. "Yes," we called back. "And tomorrow and the next day and for as long as you need us."

Lt. Colonel Carvosso Gauntlett reported in the same United States Central territory *War Cry* that "A number of Salvationists have been killed or injured in the latest raids on the Midlands. Damaged Army properties now number 150."

Catherine wrote in her "London Letter" of January 4, 1941: "Our working men's hotel is near one of the biggest underground stations in the city, where we serve 10,000 cups of tea a night." On a Monday evening, Catherine came directly from the office to take on the all–night watch shift at a first aid post started by one of the officers from the slums. This post provided a desperately needed life–saving service:

> I came away before daylight the next morning; but although the raid was on, the London buses were trundling away as usual. I fell asleep at the beginning of the ride, so did not hear the gunfire or anything that may have been going on, and I got to the office at about eight—and fell asleep again. I man-

aged somehow to keep going all day, but went to bed about seven. I heard the warning siren and the first gun of the night raid, but nothing else until the next morning.

The same thing happened to me on another night, and in the morning. I woke to find that a house, a three–storied place only a few doors from my flat—had been bombed, and that seven people had been killed in the basement where they had sheltered. I felt awful to think I had not known, but you got so accustomed to the noise, and you simply can't keep on going without sleep. I can't anyway.

One night they dropped a "Molotoff basket" in our street, and there was an incendiary bomb in nearly every garden except ours. I looked out of the window to find five huge fires burning—there at the bottom of the street and two on either side. The flat next door to my own was burning from the top, but they got the fire out very quickly.

I go down to the underground shelter to serve refreshments every week—that is, to the one nearest to where I live. I enjoy the contact with the people. They are wonderful and lovable.

Sharing the page with Catherine's "London Letter" of January 4, 1941, Carvosso Gauntlett reported that General George Carpenter, with Mrs. Carpenter, had spent a day in the Midlands, in places where there was heavy bombing. They viewed mobile canteen teams at work among crowds and a number of damaged halls and quarters. They also met the mayor of Coventry at his council chambers, which had been gutted. The Salvation Army hall was in service as a canteen, as well as a base for the distribution of clothing. Thus, many Salvationists, from the General to the rank and file of corps and social centers, became vitally and even dangerously involved in their compassionate and practical aid to victims of the blitz. Catherine was only one of many. Though a pacifist, she was serving at the battle's front line, like an enlisted soldier.

It was not long after the editor in chief had written in the American *War Cry* of blitz damage to United Kingdom Army properties that his own department at International Headquarters came under fire, and incendiary bombs rained on the annex that housed *The Young Soldier, The Deliverer* and *The Warrior*. Their offices, with equipment, files and copy, went up in smoke, before the inadequate stirrup pumps could go into action.

The War Cry of February 8, 1941 announced: "Readers of *The Young Soldier, The Warrior* and *The Deliverer* who call upon their respective editors will find them in new quarters, not far from the old haunts. They were recently blitzed out of the snug little corner which housed them for so long."

From their new window, viewing the blackened ruins open to the sky of their top floor, *The Deliverer* editor observed in the March/April 1941 issue: "We were thankful that the flames had spread no farther, that unscathed editorial comrades could make room for us. There is an even wider view of London's river, gray or shining, from the new window than from the old—and spring is coming!"

The raids continued to claim casualties in personnel and property. On Saturday night, May 12, 1941, in one of the worst of the London raids, the Army's tall International Headquarters, enveloped in the flames, finally collapsed—a total loss and a great sorrow to Salvationists everywhere.

Some of the editorial staff moved right away, more conveniently near the Army's printing works in St. Albans. The others remained in London. In his biography of Carvosso Gauntlett, Frederick Coutts recounts the tragedy as it affected the editorial and literary departments:

> Next morning "Car" stood with his comrades in the street outside the wreck of "101." So far as his departments were concerned, every file, every galley proof, every sheet of notepaper, every pen and pencil—save for a small stock at St. Albans—had gone. For some weeks, the editors ran their papers from their homes, maintaining contact with each other through their resourceful head.

The two departments moved once more, this time to 224 Upper Thames Street. Anything less was unimaginable. It was a decrepit, three–story building. Next door was a rough–and–ready restaurant that catered to truck drivers who, having traveled through the night, came in for wartime breakfast. Catherine preferred this somewhat dingy setting to a superior tea–room around the corner, confessing through her pseudonym, "Nothing is especially clean, and the cups are—well, mugs. But Ethelburga won't have her tea anywhere else."

In an essay, Catherine wrote:

> Even after the office building was no more than a few brick foundations, some of us had to remain in the center of the city. A ramshackle building in Upper Thames Street served as shelter, though it still remains a mystery how this fragile structure withstood the blast of bombs. Its flimsy walls creaked in the wind; its staircase shook under the lightest tread. Some of us contacted rats. When they suddenly shot a head through a crevice and stared enquiringly at us, it was difficult to report them to the authorities when a piece of cheese seemed a small reward for their bravery. One of the girls made the mistake of putting fish on the windowsill for the gulls. Thereafter we were

attended by a white–winged throng, who treated us night and day to an any-thing–but angelic song.

Our best contacts, though, were made at a cafe left standing among the dust and bricks, its lopsided windows overlooking a small graveyard whose headstones were either broken or tilting at all angles among weeds as tall as trees. Here, long distance lorry drivers used to come at all hours of the day, weary, dirty and cold. We went because the tea, though weak and sweetened with saccharin, was piping hot. Soon we were going because we liked the men. In the cafe by the river, the big, grimy–faced fathers quietly discussed the long–term effect of evacuation on their children. Their words had a rough wisdom. One man from a working–class district in South London said when his little girl came home, he was going to have to live a different sort of life. It seemed she had been evacuated for some time, but had come home for a few days. "You know," he said, "that kid is nicely spoken now—acts nice, too. We'd like her to stay that way." He told how the child had set such a high value on going to church that, on Sunday morning, he had taken her, "carry-ing her little hymn book and all." He hadn't gone into the church because "me and the missus never have; but we want her to keep on going."

In another autobiographical incident told through Ethelburga, humor again shines through Catherine's writing titled, "Who Needs an Incendiary Bomb when Ethelburga Is Sizzling Sausages?"

Ethelburga was asked to help a Salvationist friend at one of the Army's canteens. Hearing that the work was physically strenuous and that helpers needed to be somewhat sturdy physical specimens, Ethelburga immediately felt this was the job for her and made her way to the canteen.

Now an Army canteen is a place where you don't go unless you are pre-pared to work without being told where to find anything or what to do with it when you have found it. You walk in, smile at the Captain's wife, who is too busy to smile back, seeing she has been frying eggs and sausages for many a long hour. Then you grab a dish cloth and begin washing piles of dishes.

Ethelburga washed dishes for many hours, seeing nothing but a bowl of soapy water and the wall in front of her, feverishly hurrying to keep up with the distant yells of "more knives," "plates," or "Give us some cups," etc.

As the hours passed, Ethelburga, who had not eaten since noon, became hungrier and hungrier and more and more enamored of the savory–smelling sausages that the captain's wife was handing out. They were being cooked in a huge frying pan filled with sizzling fat. "It's the pan being full of fat that makes them come out so nice," she said victoriously, as though she had dis-covered the last word in secret weapons. Ethelburga decided on sausages for her next meal at home—with almost disastrous consequences!

Visualize a frying pan, brimful of fat, first smoking, then blazing almost to the ceiling and cast from her top–story window into the garden below!

Who needs an incendiary bomb when Ethelburga sets her mind on sizzling sausages?

Further revealing anecdotes flowed from Catherine's adventures of Ethelburga:

"It's absolutely no good," says Ethelburga, "going down to the office with a good story, because everyone has a better tale to tell."

Ethelburga's flat is a top one. She says, rather condescendingly, that if her safety were threatened, she would go down to the Anderson shelter below. But the funny thing is that Ethelburga's safety, according to her, never is threatened. To her friends, who hoped that at least she would not stay up there alone, she offered the exasperating reply that if you were bombed, it wouldn't make any difference whether you were alone or with 20 people.

One night as the "biggest gun yet" was sending shells, swizzing through the dark, Ethelburga watched the fireworks from the window under the roof. Suddenly the whole neighborhood was lit up. She ran to the kitchen window and discovered that three large buildings were burning not many doors from her own, and that a stream of smoke was issuing from the roof of the flat next door.

"You really must come downstairs!" yelled a voice from the Anderson shelter. Ethelburga replied that she would if there was any immediate danger.

Ethelburga has talked so much about the "safe feeling" in her flat that, in search of such an unusual sensation, I accompanied her there. She led me into the kitchen, with all its cream and orange decorations, enhanced by the sun setting behind an autumn–clad tree. The guns at that moment seemed to be exploding in unison. The house quivered and rocked.

"Lovely, isn't it?" asked Ethelburga.

"What? Those guns?" I said.

"No, the sunset."

The guns popped; something sinister whizzed downward. "It would be a pity if this flat were to be bombed—it is so charming," I said.

"Would you rather have tea than coffee?" asked Ethelburga, putting on the kettle.

The other morning, Ethelburga arrived at the office looking white and heavy–eyed. I was not surprised when she said she had a "perfectly awful night," for we all had.

"Ah," I thought, not without triumph, "She is affected by the raids, though she won't admit it." Aloud I said, "Air raids?"

"Gracious no!" she answered, as though I had mistaken double pneumonia for measles. "Mice!"

It was my turn to say, "Gracious!"

"You see," she went on, "a few bombs fell in our street and I thought I would make some coffee for the rescue party. I went into the kitchen and there were two mice—on the stove! It was such a shock; I couldn't sleep a wink afterward."

During the day I heard many people telling Ethelburga about their bombs; and in the first sentence of her reply, I invariably heard the word "mice." At least Ethelburga did have a better story than the rest.

A letter from Caughey Gauntlett, as Catherine's forty–eighth birthday drew near, shows the mutually caring and thoughtful relationship that existed between the Gauntletts and Catherine:

> Dear Auntie Cath, knowing your birthday is on Tuesday, I hasten to send my very sincere good wishes and congratulations. The fact that you have lived all these years is probably due to good luck rather than being due to your looking after yourself! Seriously though, I am glad that you are so much better now. I would also like to say a very personal word of appreciation of your intense interest in me and Marjorie, and your great kindness to us. I have appreciated it more than I can say. Much love to you. Caughey and Marjorie.

Four booklets by Catherine Baird were published in 1944, relating the lives and ministry of Salvationist stalwarts: *William Stevens* (Jesu Ratnam), *Little Doctor* (Harry Andrews), *Noel Hope* (Sarah L. Morewood) and *Pierrot on Wings* (Earl Ellis). The following year, the great war came to an end with the surrender of Germany in May and Japan in August. Catherine's world, although scarred by war, would return to a more settled and calm atmosphere.

Catherine Baird's pen was indeed a multi–edged sword. She used it to inspire by vivid mystical poetry, and amuse with accounts of Ethelburga's adventures, keeping a silver lining on the dark war clouds. Her pen flowed with great feeling whenever she wrote of human sorrow, suffering and stalwart spirits.

Following a visit to devastated Germany in the aftermath of the war, Catherine described the plight of children she met.

> A thin, nervous little boy—the first of 60 who arrived with him—clinging to the hand of a German nurse, entered the door of the Sunnyside Children's Home and looked up shyly at the words over the doorway, written in English and in German: "Love rules this home; faith is our support; peace is our master; happiness is our aim."
>
> Once this building, several miles from Hamburg, had been a fashionable holiday residence, overlooking the beautiful River Elbe. It is easy to hear, in imagination, orchestral music and the quiet hum of voices on the balcony, as guests take refreshment there while watching the waves gently splashing on

the sands, as they did before the war plunged the world into misery. Now, only the river moves as of yore. The city of Hamburg lies in ruins.

Today, the guests of the hotel, which has been rechristened the "Sunnyside Children's Home," are boys and girls, aged six to fourteen, who are ill from starvation. For them, the beautiful building was offered by its owners to The Salvation Army relief team in Hamburg. The children, discovered through visitation or selected from visitors of the Army's clinic, usually arrive at the home in rags and are very thin. Children in Germany today are the chief victims of the war. I saw children maimed for life through injuries received during the bombings, and since the bombings when they had chanced on a booby trap or a mine in an uncleared field.

At the Sunnyside Children's Home, those who come now know what the sign "Love rules this home" means. The university also sends students, two at a time, to spend a period of training in the home. In the visitors' book, presented to the matron, is this inscription: "You came here as conquerors, you are remaining as friends. Once you leave, you will be adored by the children you have cared for. You have shown us that love and faith are stronger than hate. We thank you. German Welfare Committee."

DEFENSE

When the wild hurricane of hate has swept
Beyond our reach the fences we had built
To keep our dear possessions quite secure;
When little heaps of ruins mark the place
Where sheltered once we hid from suffering
And boldly talked of our defended peace—
Shall we, with nothing, yet with everything,
Pass "through the needle's eye" discovering
An undefended kingdom? Shall we know
All things hate claimed from us were false—all left
By her were true and indestructible?

Was our abode a covered lodge wherein
Our unused wings had lost their power to raise
Us higher than the ceiling of our "home?"
E'en when, with passing courage, we once peered
Through bars, our careful hands had neatly forged,
Did we withdraw with fearful trembling from
The breadth and height and depth and length we saw?

Now will our sorrow lead us firmly from
The clutch of earth to loneliness and heav'n;
Now will our flutt'ring wings spread out, grow strong,
And bear us while we point our onward course;
Now shall we take the unsafe way, at last,
Unarmed and unprotected, save with God!

8

KINDRED SPIRITS

Some years after the war, Catherine explained to a session of conference delegates the origin of her poem, "Calling More Fools."

This comes very near home to you because you have had Dr. Sidney Gauntlett here this morning. This poem was written about his father, Carvosso Gauntlett. His father was a noble fool. He did not care about anything except winning people for God, and about trying to do the will of Jesus. He went to Germany when the war was over and he died in Germany. He need not have gone back to Germany; the General would have let him stay here, but he chose to go over there because after the war, Germany was in a terrible condition. I was over there in 1946, and it was really heartbreaking seeing the Army halls that had been bombed.

He was a very clever man. He spoke five languages fluently. He was not ambitious as a Salvation Army officer. He was offered promotion to Lt. Commissioner when he went over to Germany, and he refused to take the rank because there were officers over there who were older than he was and they were not commissioners. I do not think he would have died if he had remained in England, but he died in Germany. He was a fool—"a noble fool."

Calling More Fools

We are fools for Christ's sake (1 Cor. 4:10 RSV).

Passing beyond the worldly wise
He toiled, with bright, unguarded eyes,
Seeking to bring the lost
Homeward at any cost.

We gave our gold His poor to feed,
We smiled on every selfless deed,
We cheered, applauding, when He bled;
"He is a noble fool!" we said.
Clutching our gilded crowns,
Holding our dear renowns.

Sheltered, we sorrowed when He fell
Outside our cozy citadel,
Offering more gold, more bread
In memory of the dead.
But where His life–blood stains the sod
Sore wounded works His Shepherd God,
Calling more fools to seek the lost,
Fools who will pay the highest cost,
For only blood avails,
Only the Blood prevails!

One of Catherine Baird's most intriguing characteristics was her remarkable open–handedness. She lived by the principle, "Tis loving and giving, that makes life worth living."

There were several visitors to Catherine's home whom she surprised with an impromptu gift from a cabinet or a cupboard, to be long treasured. In 1978, Commissioner Paul du Plessis shared an evening meal with Catherine in her London apartment. He recalls, "She asked about my wife and family. They were in Zambia. 'Please take something to [your wife],' she said and, in spite of my protests, took a delightful little teapot from a dining–room cupboard, put it in a plastic bag and handed it to me. It remains one of our little treasures."

"There's no point in giving things to Auntie Cath," was the Gauntlett family's good–natured comment. "She'll only give them away!" Sidney and Jean Gauntlett were just amused—not surprised—when they spotted the bone china mug they had given to Auntie Cath adorning their daughter's kitchen!

Nevertheless, Catherine was not born with her spirit of generosity. She was very young when she felt the need to be free from inhibiting self–concern. Her childhood prayer to be unselfish, encouraged by her sister Winnie as they knelt by the old kitchen chair, had been repeatedly and beautifully answered through the years.

Catherine Baird exchanged many letters with Lt. Commissioner Arch Wiggins, Army historian and songwriter, who was a colleague of hers in the editorial department. The letters reveal her high estimation of Wiggins through the years, and are typical of her ongoing concern and value of her esteemed colleagues.

July 14, 1947, Dear A.R.W.—I thoroughly enjoyed your bracing letter, especially the bit about my cousin. I am so glad you have met her. I am glad you have run into a better paper situation. It is a headache and now we hear again [that] we are going back to four pages.

The farewell of Colonel Gauntlett was sad, but great. To be so believed in is a kind of reward that beats any other. We shall never cease to miss him, but we do believe he is God's man for Germany. After seeing the sorrow there, I think so, too. I wish I could go also.

Oh, at the music board the other day, the British commissioner asked me to tell you that at the national youth rally, the young people had stood with raised hands and had sung your "Thou Art the Way." He said he did not think he had ever felt so stirred.

December 16, 1947, Dear Colonel—Thank you for your three letters. First, the one about poetry. I am so glad you are so fond of us that you will not raise any further objections to our queries. You see, it is because we think a lot of you that we raise the queries at all. When a really good song comes up at the board, as you well know, one is more than thankful—and I thought this was a really good song—but that those few words were not really like you.

I appreciate very much what you say, although you know me well enough to know that the friendship and love of the people I respect is more [dear] to me than a promotion could possibly be.

Since I told you that the paper situation was a bit easier, it has again become harder. We had a sixteen–page Christmas *Young Soldier* all made up when word came through that it had to be cut down to eight pages. So, I made it into two eight–page Christmas issues. Our circulation is now 210,000. I was very grateful to you for printing that story about the German children. I had [received] a nice letter from Mrs. Carpenter about it.

I should be very glad if you would either write yourself, if you have the time, or get someone to write stories or articles that are typically Australian—the work in the Outback, for instance. You have other kinds of work over there which would be very interesting to the young folk here.

I hope you have a lovely Christmas. We shall be thinking of you, and we shall certainly miss you at our party.

September 6, 1949, Dear Archie—Yes, it is quite true that things are getting better here in the clothes and food line. Clothing is off the ration now, and that is a great help. I am personally very grateful for the parcels my brother sends me from America, because we are still short of fats and meat.

You speak about the song "Jesus Himself Drew Near." I think the chorus "Thou Art the Way" to the tune of "Finlandia" rings all around the world. We hear the cadets singing it, and the British commissioner loves it and always has it when he has gatherings of young people.

Now about your remarks concerning the music board. Of course there is nobody there who feels the least [bit] antagonistic towards you, and you ought to know this. You know that I am the only new person on the board, and that I am your friend and not your enemy. Naturally, whenever I look at a song now, I look at it from a different angle than I did before I was on the board. In those days, you often complained that I was not critical enough.

It is not like you, as an experienced song–writer, to be resentful of any suggestion made by the board. My own songs come up and are duly criticized by the board, as they always have been. If you were an amateur, you could say, "I will not alter any word, in any song of mine, until I am convinced of its necessity." But you are not an amateur, and I think your attitude is therefore a little strange. As a matter of fact, I am really quite shocked. It doesn't seem like you at all.

Please give my love to Mrs. Wiggins. God bless you both.

September 4, 1950, Dear Archie—I thought you would rejoice to know that I had [received] a letter from 2nd–Lieutenant Robert Reeve, to say they had your song ["Christ Is the Way"], which I published in the Congress issue of *The Warrior* [August 1950], mimeographed and sung one Sunday evening, with the result that, while they were singing the second verse, someone in the congregation rose and came to the penitent form. I know this will mean more to you than all the praise in the world.

For more than 45 years, the signature of "Moss" appeared in all kinds of Salvation Army publications. James Moss traced God's distinct guidance leading up to his meeting of Catherine Baird, his acknowledged mentor of the years. Moss, who passed away in 2001, spoke warmly and often about the woman who was both editor and friend to him.

Following military service in Egypt, a four–year scholarship became available to Moss, ensuring his training as an artist. But Jim still wished to become a Salvation Army officer. Although an interview with the candidates' secretary of the day confirmed an opening for him in the training college, the interviewer did not understand why Jim would not pursue his four–year degree prior to officer training. This was only until Jim told him the degree was training to become an artist.

"I don't see where The Salvation Army would use an artist!" the surprised and dismayed interviewer exclaimed.

"There and then, rightly or wrongly," Moss said, "I gave my [candidate's] star back!" He studied at the Borough Polytechnic School of Art until June 1952. It was not until his senior year that Senior–Captain Phyllis Sandover of the editorial department pointed Jim to the next door to open. "You really ought to go and see Catherine Baird," she said.

"Who is Catherine Baird?" Jim asked.

"The editor of *The Young Soldier*," she replied.

"I was amazed at what they were doing up there," Jim discovered, "the very things I'd been training for! I clicked straight away with that woman."

Catherine Baird believed in Moss, although some thought him outrageous or arrogant. She and Jim would have long talks together about his home, work, ideas, about The Salvation Army and his future. Catherine became Jim's mentor.

Moss explained: "When I first came on the building her office was an oasis for me. Catherine saw what I was trying to do and saw that I was sincere about it. Others thought I was a way–out geezer! I had to fight my way into this movement, but she was there, backing me and saying, 'Come on, let's do this.' She gave me scope, gave me opportunity to do things. [Catherine would say,] 'You're the artist—do it!' And on the strength of that, I went home and did it!"

Jim said of Catherine, "She was so feminine: very caring, very interested in what was going on. She was no fool; she had a good brain and was very well read. All these things showed. One could only respect the lady. She met you on your own level, eye to eye. There was a naturalness about her. She wouldn't give way to the hierarchy. She stood up to them!"

A new comic character was needed in *The Young Soldier*, and "Bram" was created in 1953. In some circles, there was temporary concern that a youngster of Bram's lovable naivete bore such an honored Salvation Army name. Bramwell was the first name of the Army's second General. But the new Bram fast became an international favorite, and one day General Bramwell Booth's son, Commissioner Wycliffe Booth, reassured Jim that the fictional young Bram was quite acceptable!

Bram remained a popular character in *The Young Soldier* for years. An eighty–page anthology of cartoons, "*Bram of* The Young Soldier" was published in 1980.

Catherine Baird was a loyal supporter of the cartoon's creator. "Gentle she appeared," Moss said, "but she stuck her head on the block a few times over me!

"Today, *The Young Soldier* has adapted to the changes of technology and attitudes—the editor getting his message over through the colorful, illustrated content with which the modern youngster is familiar," stated Moss. One wonders how Catherine Baird would have viewed and approached today's high tech, color cartoon strip age. Without doubt, she would have studied to keep abreast of modern techniques and used them, without the surrender of her professional principles. As her protégé James Moss survived and succeeded in the modern editorial scene, his mentor would certainly not have lagged behind.

"I thought I was rather special to her," he said. Gradually it dawned on him that others felt the same. He admitted, "She loved everyone." Moss realized that Catherine had a remarkable capacity to give and receive love, and that her concern for him was not diminished because of her genuine care for others.

Catherine's concern for others, coupled with her ever–present sense of fun, often delivered a well–timed blessing. When Lieutenant Margit Gauntlett was plowing a lone furrow as a young officer in a small corps, she received among her birthday greetings two unusual letters, supposedly dispatched from heaven. One was from her once–owned cat Sooty, the other from Pat, her dog, which had been a gift from Auntie Cath. Cherished by Margit for years, facsimiles of these letters appeared in a book, *Our Colonel*, created by members of the Balham corps congregation in memory of Catherine as part of Margit's tribute.

> Dear Margit, Many happy returns of August 15. You will be pleased to know that I do not catch birds any more. Pat and I and some other cats and dogs run a tea and coffee stall for birds, so that we can give them hot drinks before they start out for earth. You know, of course, that up here part of their job is to take angels' messages to the world on dark nights when Salvation Army lieutenants are holding open air meetings, selling *The War Cry*, or feeling lonely.
>
> We are building a nice house for you on the Gauntlett site. A few months ago, terrific loads of bricks kept coming up from earth—all for Margit Gauntlett's house. We found out that this was because of all the parcels you and the cadets sent to Germany.
>
> Pat and I are very happy and both wish you millions of years of joy. "Sooty Gauntlett."

Another editorial colleague who benefitted from Catherine's tremendous influence was Lily Sampson. From the age of sixteen, Sampson had been strongly influened by Catherine Baird in her life, objectives, zeal, and in "three privileged years [when they worked] together at International Headquarters."

Sampson's parents were Australian officers who had known and respected the Baird family since William Baird was their divisional commander and Catherine was eight years old. Sampson described Catherine's "Christlike daily life" as "flowing naturally like a spring in the meadow, refreshing all who saw it," and paid tribute to her "cheerful, unassuming, skillful handling of her work."

Sampson and another colleague, Major Gladys Taylor, created a series for *The Young Soldier* called "The Pin People," based on a children's book Taylor had written. Catherine would join in their laughter as they reviewed the escapades of the characters.

"If Catherine Baird approved it, it was with careful examination. The department respected her reactions," Sampson explained. "With her, criticism took the form of helpful suggestion and approval underlined special niceties she had seen. Sensitive herself, she gave each [staff member] the compliment of believing him the same. I loved her. She was so like Jesus."

Catherine Baird maintained a very active correspondence with many who were blessed by her friendship and encouragement. In that company were a few who were special to her—rare, kindred spirits, with open hearts and well–informed, fertile minds—with whom Catherine could share her thoughts. Such relationships were enriching and supremely supportive to all parties. One such kindred spirit was Kathleen Kendrick, a major who was working at the Army's Howard Institute in what is now Zimbabwe. Catherine met Kendrick on homeland furlough from South Africa, and bonded with her instantly. They were to remain friends throughout her life. Catherine felt that she could express herself quite honestly with Kathleen, as is evident from a 1955 letter:

> Dear Kathleen: We have had a most lovely autumn and sometimes, looking at the ethereal appearance of trees with burning leaves thinned out by the winds, I've felt this beauty to be a promise of some greater beauty beyond time. I am glad you tell your people that they don't always recognize the great among them. You know I sometimes hear members of the department saying we have no brilliant people among us and my answer to them is the one you

give your boys. They were saying it twenty years ago when Coutts, Woods and Gauntlett were being held back in little jobs because some fathead could not part with something he could not do. The great are always with us. We need not more great men, but keener sight to discern what is before us.

When news broke that Frederick Coutts was appointed territorial commander of the Australian Eastern territory, Catherine again felt free to vent to her friend her concerns and care for the new leader:

> How entirely I agree with your comments about the training college principal [Lt. Commissioner Frederick Coutts]. My one thought is that he is a great man concerned with God's will and that God's will is going to be done regarding his future, whatever shallow thinkers may devise. I am certain that the Army is in God's hands, too. We are hating the thought of seeing the Coutts family off. I hear there will be a big crowd at the station. No wonder. There may be an even bigger crowd when he returns!

Catherine Baird's suggestion to Kathleen that the crowds would be greater to greet Frederick Coutts on his return from Australia proved prophetic. In October 1963 when Commissioner Coutts returned to London, a vastly larger crowd, including a band and a hired ferry, were present to welcome him as General–elect, soon to take worldwide charge of The Salvation Army.

Coutts was obviously Catherine's choice for the nomination. Her university mentor marked her essay as "quite brilliant," in its thinly–veiled reference to her admired leader. It provides a graphic cameo of The Salvation Army's international leader:

> The Introvert has a "lean and hungry look." His long, narrow face always wore a withdrawn expression. His steely eyes bored into all who talked with him; but he rarely made more than a few casual remarks. Sometimes when he returned home from work, his wife and daughters would ask: "Anything happened at the office today?" and he would reply aggravatingly: "To be sure; we all got on with the job."
>
> When he did speak, however, what he said (whether it concerned a parable in the New Testament or a current problem) instantly touched the core of the matter, leaving us wondering why we had hitherto been so slow of understanding.
>
> The Introvert ploughed a lonely furrow, being a kind of pioneer in his particular circle, examining accepted doctrines and beliefs so that a silent revolution in thought took place in the annual text books prepared by him. His influence was worldwide, especially among the young. He answered all criticisms, but never apologized for his views nor cared what they might cost him.

At board meetings, the Introvert appeared uninterested while other members quibbled over trivialities or introduced irrelevant subjects. Suddenly, when everyone seemed to be drowning in muddled thinking, he would uncoil his long, spare figure like a huge caterpillar and, in a few well chosen words, bring order out of chaos, rescuing the grateful chairman.

Among the young he had a large following; among reactionaries, many enemies. He made no intimate friends, yet in choosing the right person for a special post, his judgment was unerring.

It would appear to me that the power of the Introvert will remain, and that the most worthwhile activity in time is achieved by those whose introversion leads them beyond both time and space.

WHEN JESUS LOOKED

When Jesus looked o'er Galilee,
So blue and calm and fair,
  Upon her bosom, could He see
A cross reflected there?

When sunrise dyed the lovely deeps,
And sparkled in His hair,
  O did the light rays seem to say:
A crown of thorns He'll wear?

When in the hush of eventide,
Cool waters touched His feet,
  Was it a hymn of Calvary's road
He heard the waves repeat?

But when the winds triumphantly
Swept from the open plain,
  The Master surely heard the song:
The Lord shall live again!

9

SEARCHER AFTER TRUTH

O f her 42 years' active service, Catherine Baird spent 30 as editor of *The Young Soldier*, in Chicago from 1923 to 1934, and in London from 1934 to 1953. Before she relinquished her editorship, the circulation of the paper had expanded to 260,000 in the United Kingdom alone.

Much had happened since William Booth decided that young people should have their own newspaper and launched the first edition of *The Little Soldier* in 1881. This newspaper would later be called *The Young Soldier*. During the Second World War, the office of *The Young Soldier* in London was destroyed by fire twice. For months, the editorial office was a suitcase carried by its homeless editor, Catherine Baird. Nevertheless, the presses hummed and parcels of *Young Soldiers* bearing peaceful news were dispatched to all parts of the world.

Among those who inherited the editorship of the international *Young Soldier* from its founding editor Captain John Roberts were Commissioner Mildred Duff (1896–1926) who later became one of the Army's noted writers, and the first editor's daughter Brigadier Ethel Roberts (1926–1934). Upon Brigadier Ethel Roberts' marriage, Adjutant Catherine Baird became successor to the distinguished line.

To homes not acquainted with the Bible, *The Young Soldier* conveyed God's Word. The local bar patron, taking the paper home for his child, could read the weekly Bible story presented at the Army's Company Meeting (Sunday school). This little paper winged its way around the world. Today its name has been changed to *Kids Alive*, and it includes readers of the Army's Postal Sunday School—those not able to attend The Salvation Army—with participants in Eastern Europe, Israel and Africa. The updated and colorful modern style of the paper is a dramatic change from the black and white production of Catherine's time, but the power pulsating in it has inspired the paper since its inception in 1881.

In July 1947, in addition to her responsibilities as editor of *The Young Soldier*, Catherine Baird accepted the editorship of *The Warrior*. As its title implies, this compact magazine, issued monthly, served to encourage and prepare the youthful Salvationist.

One of two photographs appearing in the American *War Cry* of May 1, 1953 depicted Colonel Frederick L. Coutts, with the announcement that General Albert Orsborn had appointed him as principal of the international training college in London. The colonel, well known for his literary expertise, had made an official tour of American centers the previous year. As time elapsed, his notable backroom work of many years and public American tour prepared Coutts for a more prominent role—a role that would ultimately lead to his generalship of the worldwide Army.

The other photo was that of his editorial colleague and successor, Lt. Colonel Catherine Baird, the newly appointed literary secretary. She was recognized in the report as "one of the Army's foremost writers." Speaking in retrospect, her friend and future successor, Commissioner Kathleen Kendrick, said:

> When Colonel Baird was made the Army's literary secretary, it was an appointment widely welcomed. The Salvation Army had not always made appointments so appropriate, but now it was placing a poet—its foremost poet—in the literary chair. She could bring only grace and distinction to that office, as she undoubtedly did.

The literary secretary headed the work of the Army's literary department, as distinct from the editorial department, and oversighted the annual production of new books and recurring editions of *The Salvation Army Year Book*, *The Officer*, *The Soldier's Armory*, the *International Company Orders* (a yearly textbook for leaders and teachers in the Army's Sunday schools) and missionary literature. Manuscripts submitted for publication were perused by the literary secretary and appropriate recommendations made to the relevant board or council. Until reorganization in 1990, overseas territories submitted manuscripts to International Headquarters for approval. The literary secretary read and assessed submitted manuscripts for the guidance of the Chief of the Staff, on whose authority permission to publish would be granted.

In 1952 Catherine Baird was appointed literary secretary to the General, with promotion to the rank of full colonel. Lt. Colonel Harry Dean, who as a senior–captain joined the department in 1953, recalls:

> She was my boss from then on—until her retirement. We became great friends. Those years were spent in adjacent offices, discussing the work in which I was engaged, books that were exciting us, having theological and other insights. It was interesting and enriching. Early on, she became a close friend of Margaret's [Mrs. Dean] and always took an interest in our two sons.
>
> She was gentle, but not weak. There was a quiet strength about her. On matters of principle she was immovable. She would stand up against authority if need be. On one particular issue, she repeatedly said a quiet no to one of the generals under whom she served. He just had to give way. No sparks flew, but she gained her point.

Lt. Colonel William Burrows, who was associated with Catherine Baird through his literary work, wrote:

> Her welcome gift to me when I came to the department was a large, beautifully dressed doll for my little daughter. Several years afterwards, when I was to undergo a very serious operation, she paid personally for me to see a specialist. Since she was my "boss" at the time, she negotiated for our family and quarters to be nearer to headquarters to save me complications in traveling.
>
> She was not perfect, but as near perfect as we could conceive, for her love for Jesus embraced conceptions of God which matched and could challenge a modern age. We lesser mortals simply stand to attention and salute.

From July 1952 until her retirement—delayed by two years—in September 1957, Catherine Baird filled the influential post of literary secretary with credit. Throughout her tenure at International Headquarters, Catherine's literary output was not confined to *The Young Soldier, The Warrior* or her other publications. Her articles appeared in the Army's United Kingdom periodicals and overseas territories. The United States *War Cry* presented a copious selection of her writings over the years.

Her work, particularly in the United Kingdom, did not always appear under her own name. At the time, editorial staff made a practice of using pen names, imposed or chosen. Sometimes a mere "C.B." would identify her work. Catherine often wrote anonymously of her own family, friends or colleagues. Sometimes her identity was fairly obvious; in other cases it was obscure. Her characters and champions were real people, regardless what she called them in essays or articles.

Even Catherine Baird's essays, written in retirement during her study at the University of London, deal only with real life characters and issues. Catherine's tutor, Dr. F. E. England, though unaware of the identities of her characters, habitually marked her papers with comments like "excellent," and "fascinatingly interesting." Her essay selection indicated the wide range of her interest, clarity of thought and sheer zest for everyday life—things important and trivial. She seasoned her writing with her own brand of fun, by which the ordinary takes on a certain sparkle.

In Catherine's lifelong commitment to education, teaching and philosophy, the following excerpts from one of her essays reveal her own diligent search for truth, going beyond her initial induction to the Christian faith.

> Though of course education begins in childhood, it never ends. The insatiable curiosity of many sends them to institutes, universities, clubs etc. The teacher has to be in love with the knowledge he possesses before he can take the pains necessary to impart it to others. Not all are blessed with the insatiable curiosity which makes learning exciting. Perhaps teachers are like poets—born, not made. They should indeed have adequate training, better conditions, higher pay; but none of these things will make them into educators. Naturally, the genuine teacher would like his honest needs supplied, but if not, he will still go on teaching.
>
> Rabidranath Tagore said: "Teaching is like knocking at the door of the mind." Can anything be more satisfying than hearing the hinges creak and seeing the door swing open? Unless it be the moment given to those who hear the knock and begin to venture, perhaps timidly, into the vastness beyond the door.
>
> The answer to the question "Why do you study philosophy?" has to be personal. Assuming that, more than love of wisdom, philosophy is the search for truth about reality—can anyone bypass it altogether?
>
> The child's feet dancing over the African veld seemed freer than her thoughts, always shepherded back to the fundamentalist fold. Her eyes, so small, scanned vast areas of purple–tinted hills, out of all proportion to the minute physical organs, yet her reflective faculty must be ordered into the 11 points of doctrine subscribed to by all Salvationists. They would not stay there. First they moved gingerly toward a study of the Bible, in the light of higher criticism. This path led gently to a look at religions other than [that of] the Hebrews and at philosophies which, at root, had a resemblance to religious faith. How could she or anyone work out a faith to live by without sitting at the feet of the wise and letting all she had been taught [be analyzed] as through a winnowing process? A great deal of excess baggage had to be cast aside; but what was left came alive with new significance and beauty.

The scientist delving into the secrets of the material universe may not be a philosopher, but would he not be a better scientist if he were also a philosopher? It has been said that the botanist dissecting a flower sees in it less than does the poet. But why should this be? Wouldn't the poet be a better poet if he also knew what the botanist knows? And will the botanist remain satisfied with naming parts? Will not the poet and the botanist meet somewhere, sometime having come by different routes to the same place?

Men with insatiable curiosity about the world they see and touch have, it would seem to me, much in common with the philosopher. Perhaps both are looking for reality.

The only barrier to learning, through the gospel [and] more about the nature of God and His will, must be the closed mind, or that one so cluttered up with set ideas that there is no room for any new flash of light, often revealed through Christian scholars. The childlike approach of wonder and of everlasting questioning and seeking is always rewarded by fresh insight until the seeker, gradually developing, can see more and more of the vast love which shall replace all other powers.

A Blind Man Prays

I pray for courage to receive the light,
When with amaze and awful fear, I find
In truth's resplendent blaze
Old thoughts, old ways, old creeds
Must be abandoned with all haste; for they—
Accepted once with mild credulity
As hiding places for my furtive soul—
Though pretty castles, were not built by God.

One man is robbed of sight by grim disease,
Another shuts his eyes and turns from light.
Both are bereft of beauty; both are blind!
I have not known disease, but I have lived
By choice in shadowy shelters, undisturbed.
Now, drenched in loneliness, I face the dawn
And pray for courage to receive the light.

In 1990, the popular weekly *The People's Friend* carried an interesting question and answer. "Could you please tell me the origin of the name Baird?" The reply, "Baird is derived from the Gaelic 'bard,' meaning 'poet.'" If Catherine Baird ever knew how well–named she was, it is quite probable that in her characteristic modesty she would never have verbalized it. But, her works clearly do.

Catherine Baird would not have agreed with friend H. Miles that she was the Army's "only poet." She gladly recognized, appreciated and encouraged others—even a General. Some of her friends were amused when she suggested to the Army's international leader of the day, Albert Orsborn, that the God–given gift of poetry, which he powerfully proved to possess, was of supreme importance. In effect, she said to the General: "You are the head of our Army now, but it is by your songs you will be remembered." As time has passed, few relate strongly to Albert Orsborn the General, but many are blessed weekly as they sing his well–loved and uplifting spiritual songs.

It would be difficult to assess the extent of Catherine Baird's output in poetry and song writing alone. In the current edition of the Salvation Army *Song Book*, used internationally, Catherine has contributed a dozen songs in addition to a translation and an added verse. A list of her contributions to the music publications of the Army can be found in the Appendix to this book. *The Musical Salvationist* of 1927 to 1993 lists 45 songs with words by Catherine Baird, with other editions of Army music also carrying her compositions.

In addition to her three books, *Poems, The Sword of God* and *Reflections*, and contributions to other anthologies, Catherine met many requests for verses on special occasions, including corps centenaries, weddings, dedications of children and other events. Her poems appeared weekly under the heading *Our Own Bard* in the American *War Cry* during her time in Chicago. The international staff band used her lines for many years on their Christmas cards. Her "Song of Praise" (music by Leslie Condon) was written at the request of the General for the centenary celebrations in 1965. Catherine Baird's words are not only preserved in print of all kinds, but many of her songs, often sung around the world, are deeply engraved in the hearts of Salvationists.

Anticipating the High Council of 1993, where 49 leading officers met to elect the Army's next international leader, the March 20, 1993 *Salvationist* shared the reflections of two Generals who had come to the crucial moments of the High Council in which each was ultimately to be elected. Clarence Wiseman was quoted: "When in due course the president announced that I had received the requisite absolute majority and was therefore the General–elect, I had difficulty in controlling my emotions. For one dramatic moment, I needed desperately the inward assurance that my fellow–councilors had been led by God, that I could depend on His grace and strength for a task I knew to be far beyond my human competence. In that fleeting fraction of time, the Lord brought to my mind, like a shaft of light, an inspired phrase from a cherished hymn: 'I cast my load on timeless grace.' Supported by that knowledge, I left the privacy of the council chamber for the frenetic world of press, radio and television." The "cherished hymn" was penned by Catherine Baird.

Eva Burrows, retiring as General in 1993, had similar memories of the council that elevated her to international leadership. Near the end of voting at the High Council, as they prayed, the words of one of Baird's songs came to her mind, adding to her sense of peace and confidence in God:

> *Though the future is veiled*
> *Thou shalt not be afraid,*
> *For the peace of the Lord*
> *On thy heart has been laid.*

Verses sung from the heart are often means of grace and inspiration. Words, however, which spring to the surface of the soul's reservoir with such unerring accuracy and timing are surely the echo of the voice of God, born and bred in the heart and mind of the prophetic and prayerful poet, to be divinely delivered to the supplicant at the right moment—not only to prospective Generals, but to all spiritually sensitive souls.

Though previously disheartened by criticism from the London literary officer, Catherine responded to the encouragement of Commissioner Samuel Logan Brengle, and with the support of her territorial commander in Chicago, Commissioner William McIntyre, published a book of 47 poems in 1933. Her prolific pen went on to produce a number of books designed for Salvation Army readers.

In 1944 *Little Doctor* was published, relating the story of Harry Andrews, who in his single room living quarters and medical study in India was the forerunner of one of the Army's most significant and far reaching ministries. From his improvised surgery was born the great medical missionary work of The Salvation Army in India, pioneered by the "little doctor." Later, Dr. Henry John Andrews' heroism was to earn him, posthumously, the Victoria Cross. His heroism was forever memorialized in Catherine's book:

> His wiry figure could be seen running here and there, stooping over inert bodies, working swiftly so that, as soon as an ambulance was available, as many as possible could be collected from amid the flying bullets and sent off to safety.
>
> As he slid the last stretcher into its place, a burst of gunfire cracked sharply. The ambulance moved out of a cloud of smoke and started on its way

to safety. But the "little doctor" lay still, among the dead, as one overcome with weariness might lie, having fallen asleep at his work.

In 1948 she wrote *God's Harvester*, a profile of her hero, Commissioner McIntyre. In the same year, *Of Such Is the Kingdom* came off the press. This manual, written to help those who would lead young people into a Christian experience, provided practical guidance with insight into the hearts and minds of children. Her love and respect for children shines through in insights such as "Every child has three fundamental needs: love, security and significance."

In 1950 her book *The Sword of God and Other Poems* brought fifty–two poems to readers, including the one that earned the book's title.

The Sword of God

God has a sword—
Out of Himself He fashioned
A weapon forged for men
At war with ill.
All hallowed was the dawn
Of Christmas morning,
When Heaven ensphered
The lowly cattle shed,
For God unsheathed His sword
and, stooping, laid it
Within the reach
Of every fighting man!

Other books that flowed from her pen included *The Friends and Other Stories*, published in 1950, a vivid and intricately crafted collection of stories for girls 11 years of age and older. *My Book of Praise and Prayer Children's Booklet*, published in 1954, expressed the hearts and minds of children in thankfulness as they contemplate the wonderful world in which they find themselves. In 1955, *The Soldier* added to the body of Catherine's books, recounting the early history of her family. *The Evidence of the Unseen* in 1956 featured eighteen devotional meditations, and in 1957 *The House of the Rock* presented lessons from the four Gospels, targeted for young readers. *With Colors Waving* sketched an anthology of Army prose. *The Ten Commandments* (1963) and *The Fruit of the Spirit* (1965) were two pamphlets presenting short Bible studies. In the latter, her insightful writing on gentleness is a reflection of her own life:

Gentleness is an expression of disciplined power. When it is named as "fruit of the Spirit," gentleness cannot be equated with a quiet voice, a noiseless step, a soft touch or a docility that may flatter our egos when we meet it. Nor must gentleness be confused with timidity or the kind of amiability in those who, having no settled convictions based on faith in God, agree with all men readily. Christian gentleness derives from knowledge and possession of the power that is in Christ. As this power has revolutionized the world, so it transforms the whole being of him who receives it gladly. It becomes visible in courtesy where rudeness might be excused, in desire to heal when it would be easier to wound, in calm courage rather than bravado, [and] in unobtrusive consideration for others. But these characteristics are only a few signs of a deep compassion bestowed and controlled by the gentle Christ.

In 1975, Catherine Baird's book of 60 poems, *Reflections*, was released, receiving a worldwide response from appreciative readers.

IN TUNE

God sings His lyric songs among the trees,
His feet tread lightsome, where the hurrying breeze
Blows cool across the golden–daisied fields,
Or where the warm brown earth her fruitage yields.
I wander through His cornfields and His lanes,
Seeing through finite, ofttimes wistful eyes,
The hills, the dim–lit valleys and the plains,
Like grand orchestral music harmonize.
Enchanted soul, I silently commune
With Him: "Harmonious God, my heart attune!
In all this grand accord I would not be
The lonely harp whose notes discord with Thee."

10

THE WORK NEAREST
HER HEART

In September 1957, having completed 42 years of service as an officer including a two–year extension, Colonel Catherine Baird officially entered retirement. This term proved to be a misnomer.

Cradled in Salvation Army officers' quarters, she had been involved in the Army's mission since childhood. As the date of her retirement drew near, Catherine was left in no doubt as to the estimation of her colleagues. Many messages were received, often with the caliber of the senders adding weight to their words.

Catherine's retirement announcement in *The War Cry* echoed around the Army world. Pens flowed and typewriters clicked as friends and colleagues kept Catherine's Balham postman busier than usual, while they hastened to express their appreciation and good wishes.

Her old editorial colleague Colonel Percival L. DeBevoise, also in his final days of active service, greeted her from New Jersey:

> My dear Cath, The latest *Cry* from London puts me in sweet and distinguished company. So you, too, become a citizen that is called senior in September. How wonderful to be retired out of the scramble, untouched by decisions—be they wise or crazy. Time to write, read, play, converse with friends, do little kindnesses so long neglected. Time for birds, trees, the good earth, walking, thinking. I hope God gives you many years of good health to enjoy the rest you deserve. Maybe we will meet if you remain in England. You leave a wonderful influence—your words, poems, messages. Most of all, recollections of your distinctive self. You have always held a little sanctuary in the hearts of the DeBevoise family—and always will. If Elsie were here she

would join me in sending several bushels of love and wishing you the best of everything. DeBs.

In his own retirement General Albert Orsborn wrote from his home, Old Orchard, in Bournemouth:

> My dear Colonel, I suppose it is true, though to me it seems quite incredible, that you will be retiring this week from active service. You cannot go from your career and your present position without my saying once again what pure joy it has been to know and work with you. All through the years, since you became known to me through your writings, and I felt you were something more than a name, a really kindred spirit in ideals and purpose, I have held you in very high esteem.
> My experience of your work during my term as General served to confirm you in my regard. Everything you undertook was well done. I could tell your work without reading the signature. In suggesting that I write my book [autobiography, *The House of My Pilgrimage*] you raised my sights to new possibilities of service. I trust the forthcoming publication may justify your hopes and satisfy the requirements of your high standards.
> Believe me, if we meet, anywhere in the world, it will be for me and for my wife a very great joy.
> I rather hope you will still serve, as others have done, even though actually retired. With many thanks, my warmest regards and prayer that our heavenly Father may bless you. Yours sincerely, Albert Orsborn.

Lt. Colonel Gordon Avery wrote appreciatively to Catherine, particularly mentioning her part in the preparation of the Army's 1953 *Song Book*. Later, in his informative series in a 1959 edition of *The Musician*, "They Gave Us Our Song Book," he wrote:

> As a member of the international music board for 11 years, Colonel Baird rendered valuable service in the interests of Army song. She was also a valued member of the Song Book Revision Council, which prepared the present edition of the song book. Apart from her actual songs which appear in the song book, many of the others, probably more than 100, bear traces of her inspiration in those alterations and revisions which have added considerably to the beauty and usefulness of the songs in question.

Much of the burden of this edition's preparation had fallen on the shoulders of Catherine Baird's friend and predecessor, Frederick Coutts, who at the time of her retirement was recently appointed territorial commander for the Australia Eastern territory. Many years later, as he conducted Catherine's funeral service, General Coutts paid tribute to her literary prowess, and in

particular referred to their collaboration and her customary painstaking care in the preparation of the 1953 edition of the *Song Book.*
From Bombay, Mrs. Lt. Commissioner Olive L. Holbrook wrote:

> My dear Colonel, I would join the innumerable Salvationists who cannot boast a personal acquaintance, yet thank you sincerely for giving us the privilege of sharing your thoughts, set, as they reach us, in beautiful and heart–stirring language. Everything we read over your initials, or under your name or camouflaged in some not–too–successful way, whether for officers or schoolgirls, for your readers or the whosoever of the publications circulation, conveys a message skillfully. Especially in your poems, we often feel we are entering into sacred personal experiences—standing on holy ground.
>
> Then, too, how keenly we appreciate the succession of good Army books and booklets. The standard is high, and one dare not begin to enumerate, we can only say they come refreshingly for our own reading, and are much "on loan" to whet the appetite of young English–speaking Salvationists and friends.
>
> We are happy to imagine that freedom from routine may serve to facilitate the flow of inspiration; you may be at liberty to explore new sources, and follow your own "gleam."
>
> My husband shares with me both appreciation and good wishes, but he has given me the privilege of writing the letter.

As literary secretary to the General, Catherine Baird directed the work of the literary department, and was also responsible for the welfare of its officers and employees. Unavoidable were the pressures of constant creativity and forever meeting the unforgiving deadline. It was a heavy commitment for a single woman approaching 60, who would return home in the evening, sometimes to finish urgent work, before tackling endless chores involved in "looking after oneself."

Weekends needed to bring some respite if Catherine were to return to the job on Mondays with some degree of renewal. She would "special" at corps sometimes. This could be time consuming in preparation and travel, and needed to be sensibly limited. For most of her working life, Catherine had suffered from severe and quite disabling headaches. These, not surprisingly, eased only in her retirement.

Many active headquarters officers delight in and thrive on local officership in the company of the corps on weekends, and return refreshed to the headquarters routine on Monday mornings. For Catherine Baird, the emotional and mental output of the week needed more than Sunday corps attendance. Perhaps she found that God could minister to her directly in the solitude of a

Sunday spent in quietness for the renewal of her spiritual strength—even for her survival.

Catherine's limited pre–retirement attendance at the local corps was not by default but for the greatest need. To have done otherwise would have cost her more than she could afford, and all to whom she brought such spiritual enlightenment would have been infinitely poorer.

But when the literary secretary made her last official journey from International Headquarters, and as a soldier retired to Balham, she meant business, and contributed vitally for all of her long retirement years.

The built–up, busy and degenerating inner London location of Balham became Catherine's final appointment for twenty–seven years. There, as Dr. John Coutts explained in his talk on the BBC World Service in 1987, her simple home could be a refuge for the defeated and the desperate. "For her, in youth," said Coutts, "District Six was holy ground; in age it was Hosack Road, London."

Her poetry kept pace with the space age:

> *What profit should we win the race*
> *To solve the mysteries of space,*
> *And send new suns and satellites*
> *To signal through ten thousand nights? ...*
> *And what are victories of skill*
> *Unless, exploring God's will*
> *We prove the law we there have found*
> *In this our world—holy ground? ...*

None welcomed more Catherine Baird's arrival at Balham Congress Hall, or benefitted more from it, than the commanding officer, Captain Lawrence Smith, who, with his wife and daughter, arrived in May 1956, specially appointed to the corps in the challenging days of post–war rebuilding following wartime devastation. In retirement Major Smith remembers his first encounter with Catherine in the summer of that year:

> One Sunday morning, I noticed that Colonel Catherine Baird had come to worship with us. She made her way to a seat at the front. I could not resist the temptation to ask if she was coming to join us. Her response was warm and friendly, and it was quite clear that her mind was made up to become a soldier at Balham. What an asset she was! Her wealth of experience and knowledge of the Scriptures were used to full advantage.
>
> Although I have always been grateful to God for His sustaining grace during almost four years of captivity in the Far East, in Japanese prisoner–

of–war camps, the privations experienced obviously left their mark on me, mentally and physically. After serving with the Royal Army Medical Corps for more than six years it was not easy to adjust to the life of a Salvation Army corps officer, despite the certainty of my calling.

During those early years, there were occasions when I felt a need to share my feelings, but the opportunity to do so was rare. Sadly, I was to discover certain people in positions of responsibility who appeared insensitive. That was until I met Colonel Baird. I didn't look for sympathy. In fact, during my many conversations with the colonel there was no mention of "down days" or "up days." Her relationship with God was so evidently close it was a privilege to visit her in her home, which had become a sanctuary. "You are always welcome to come and spend time in the quietness of my home," she would often say to my wife and me. Its atmosphere was like that of an ante–room to heaven.

One day, my wife met with an accident in the kitchen. With a badly scalded foot, she was unable to walk about for a week or so. The compassion and care of the colonel during that time of need made a great impression on us.

On Thursday January 8, 1958 my wife and I, with our daughter Lorraine, who was nearly five years old, left Balham for Middlesbrough Central corps. Colonel Catherine Baird came to see us off at King's Cross Station. As we were about to board the train for Darlington the colonel handed us the sum of two pounds to purchase a meal en route. That was a lot of money in those days. We have often remembered that nicely served meal, and the colonel who with typical kindliness provided it.

Having been released from the official pressures of International Headquarters administration, Catherine was free to enjoy active service as a soldier in the corps at Balham. She had resolved not to become one of the "back seat critics." With this in mind, it is noteworthy that, as Major Lawrence Smith observed on her first appearance that Sunday morning at Balham Congress Hall corps, Catherine made her way to a seat at the front.

In the booklet *Our Colonel,* prepared by the Balham corps, a soldier recalled Catherine's encouragement and advice on one occasion and added: "I cannot remember all she said, but I will always remember her sweet face. I shall miss seeing her sitting in the front row, on the left–hand side of the hall."

From the many years of being "behind the lines" serving the Army from the distance of a headquarters, the aging Catherine made her way in Balham not only to the front row, but to the front line—to the "sharp end" of the war.

With only five years of officership behind her, the journey to the United States had led straight to her appointment at Chicago territorial headquarters. True to type, Catherine had busied herself when free from the office routine in the leadership and encouragement of young people, on occasional campaigns, and was always involved personally in the welfare of others. The nature of her appointments, however, dictated that the majority of her work emanated from her desk as secretary in Colonel Gauntlett's office and then as editor.

Colonel Gauntlett's grandson and namesake, Colonel Sidney Gauntlett, points out the dramatic role change of "Auntie Cath" in that transition from International Headquarters administration to the release to a wonderful ministry in Balham. From her early days at headquarters, he observes, by far the most of her ministry had been remote:

> She was private secretary to my grandfather when she first had contact with our family. That was very much behind the scenes. Then there were all these years in literary work. It was a remote ministry. In her retirement it was the one–on–one: the corps, the cake stall, people calling at her house.

For example, Sidney and his wife Jean called one day to find cadets and a courting couple having tea with Catherine. The young man played the piano while his girlfriend sang. "It was a place where they could meet each other," he said. "There was that kind of relationship with young people who found a refuge, or a healing, or somebody stimulating to talk to—whatever their need was. Then there was the launderette and the fellowship there, mostly older folk; and the neighbors. It was all close contact—'one–on–one.'"

Catherine's style of combat had changed, but her effectiveness remained. On the field, her rare ability to relate to all age groups and classes would be remarkably utilized. So on most days, her best blue uniform gave way to the Balham battle dress of the ordinary housewife, and her briefcase to a shopping bag. The memorandum of appointment for the literary secretary to the General was neatly filed away. She had retired to the front firing line.

Catherine had no dread of retirement. She recalled:

> When retirement became an imminent certainty, my colleagues and I would discuss the future. One doleful voice said, "Won't it be awful? No authority; no prestige. Our friends will drift away." However, our covenant had not been made with positions of authority, or with prestige, or even with friends, but with God. So long as one other person existed in the world, we need never be out of work.

Corps officers are always on the lookout for potential local officers—Salvationists with leadership qualities and other skills who form the volun-

tary front line force in a local corps. Catherine Baird was known internationally for her literary genius. Her friends assumed that retirement might allow
Catherine respite for a fuller flow from her pen. Also, despite her age, she had
a special affection for and understanding of the young. Yet who would blame
Captain Noel Everest, appointed to take charge of Balham Congress Hall
about three months after her retirement from International Headquarters, for
recognizing a good thing when he saw it? There is no commanding officer in
Christendom but would welcome such a "retired" into his corps. Especially
when a new Silver Threads club was to be formed and her help was needed.

Apart from her ability and personality, Catherine enhanced any situation
with her unique sense of fun. For this reason, we ought to let Ethelburga
relate her version of the entreaties, rejoinders and rationalizations between
the coaxing captain and herself which ultimately led to Colonel Catherine's
happy help in the running of the new Silver Threads program:

> My friend Ethelburga was most emphatic when the captain suggested she
> might be interested in helping at the Silver Threads club he was going to form.
> Ethelburga says we should all stick to our own line, and that she has always
> had a deep, settled conviction that her work is among the young. "A deep, set-
> tled conviction," she says, dismissing all airy–fairy chatter about mystical
> experience, "is a call." Ethelburga, I have noticed, feels all experiences except
> her own are a bit on the airy–fairy side. The captain's appealing and disap-
> pointed eyes did not move her—nor did the youthfulness of his eager face.
>
> "And another thing," continued Ethelburga, "I'm not going to be tangled
> up with petty squabbles about who will pour the tea and make the cakes."
> She reminded the captain of Bimblebrook corps, where there was a cold war
> between the Home League and the band because someone had got the
> blue–rimmed cups mixed up with the pink–rimmed Home League ones.
> Ethelburga says they all belong to the Army and she can't see what mixing
> blue– and pink–rimmed cups has to do with working for God. If anyone can
> tell her, of course, she'll be glad. Not that she will believe their explanations.
> "Squabbles and worldwide effort to win people for God just don't go togeth-
> er," she asserts.
>
> The captain agreed that they don't; but that, for this reason, folk who
> don't encourage bickering are just the sort to help with club work. He asked
> would Ethelburga at least come and give a hand at the opening. Or just talk
> to the old folk. "You mean men and women, don't you?" asked Ethelburga.
> People with silver threads in their hair don't want to be lumped together as
> "old folk," "old dears," etc. Ethelburga's hair has black threads among the sil-
> ver. She says now that she did not realize she was already taking sides with
> the Silver Threaders.

Anyway, Ethelburga had once seen the immaculate captain lift in his arms and carry, to comfort and care [for] an ill but incredibly dirty old man. She had been more impressed by this than by the captain's undeniable organizing ability and general efficiency. "He really loves that old chap," she had told herself. So now, she smiled and promised the captain, "I'll come."

Ethelburga went "for the captain's sake" to the opening day of the club. She watched the gallant company assemble, wanting nothing more than a cup of tea, fellowship with each other, some games, simple entertainment. "True, they enjoy songs of the past, but," says Ethelburga, "they have selective taste. They prefer the little girl who has spent hours practicing some of the classics and can sing for them without a single error to the lazy one who thinks anything will do. It won't." ... In their day, the Silver Threads members have enjoyed some things lovely and of good report. They still think on these things and treasure them. Now with loved ones gone and families grown up and moved away, they enjoy the club that brings them together. They are far from the anti–social types who give us trouble. These are normal, sociable folk and we have a great deal to learn from them.

Should you slyly remind Ethelburga of her "deep, settled conviction that her work is with the young," she may be slightly prickly. "So it is," she says. "This captain is young—and I'm helping him." Besides, some of the finest young folk in the corps work side by side with older ones "waiting at tables." "And," Ethelburga says, "you can't pick out a particular section and just work for that. You have to go where you are needed and you'll suddenly discover you are also doing the work nearest your heart."

Retirement may bring the opportunity for some to ease the pace. An extra hour or so in bed would seem a pleasant prospect—well–earned. Catherine Baird's daily retirement routine of bed at midnight and rising at five would seem remarkably like that which she had been used to in active service. Her niece Dorothea writes from Norway, remembering Catherine's astonishing morning ritual:

Cathy loved to go to the launderette early in the morning and do her shopping, finish her housework and then sit down either reading or writing, usually at about 10 A.M. She chuckled because some people believed she'd only just "got going."

When first appointed to Balham with her husband in 1978, Major Sheila Groom was rather mystified by the early morning promenading of Catherine:

My family could nearly set our clock most mornings when we saw Colonel Baird going past at just after 7.30 A.M. We found out that she was going to the launderette. This was puzzling. How could one person, as neat and tidy at Colonel Baird, have so much washing?

"I don't go because I have washing," explained the colonel, "but I've made friends with the elderly people who take their washing there [CB herself was 83 years old]. If I see them regularly, then I know if they become ill and I can help them." And she did. Not only with cakes and a friendly word.

So Catherine became a regular patron of the Chestnut Grove launderette to meet and enjoy her many friends. There, she would help in folding their sheets, or talk with them about their families. The clients knew little or nothing of Catherine's profession, that she was a Salvation Army colonel and a writer and poet of international repute. Incredibly, even Edna Fry, whose friendship with "Bairdie" lasted for 20 years, until Catherine's death knew nothing of her accomplishments, only learning of them at her funeral where tributes told their own stories. To the launderette customers, Catherine was simply their friend, interested in them.

A fellowship among the company of the launderette ladies developed over the years. They shared the fun and fury of daily life, releasing their tensions as they met and chatted while the machines turned. As the years passed, they gradually grew old together, inevitably suffering the loss of family and friends. One can imagine Catherine, the unofficial minister, shock–absorber and means of grace, always on hand and available, quietly supporting this hard–working, growing company in all the concerns of their extended families.

This ministry over so many years, conducted in a sense beyond the conventional Army corps program and unrecorded statistics, points to the fact that the Salvationist's influence need never be confined. As Ethelburga had said regarding the Silver Threads work, "You have to go where you are needed, and you'll suddenly discover you are also doing the work nearest your heart."

As the years took their toll, Catherine spoke of her friends at the launderette and Balham community, many of whom were years older than she, while reflecting on her own old age.

> Time has altered the area where I have lived for 46 years. Citizens who worked hard to buy their homes are now poor, aged and often handicapped. Every day as I shop or make my way to the launderette, I am amazed and humbled by their courage. Frequently I meet George, with the collapsed lung, pausing for breath as he manages to make his way to the news stand; I greet Brenda, crippled with arthritis, using her shopping basket as a support; Lucy, with her ailing dog in a child's pushchair. I stoop to stroke the shaggy, drooping head, as she tells me: "He's all I've got."

Once I could climb a mountain, sit up all night, because the day was too short for all my duties. Now I avoid even a short flight of stairs, and arrange my work in short periods, thankful that I still can do it. Besides, through the miracle of thought I can travel—no passport, no luggage, no wearisome journey—and see again the purple plush mountainside with silver leaves dancing in the sun. Better still, I can enthusiastically sponsor young friends on their charity walks, or starting out on adventure courses. I cannot carry the loads I would like to lift from my friends, but I can love them and by any possible means let them know that I care. I can make them welcome in my home, for is not that what home is for?

I must delve into a deeper search for the truth about God, revealed in Jesus Christ my Lord. This has made me relinquish the foolish attempt to shape everybody into one mold. The gardener would tell me not to try changing roses into tulips, or violets into pansies. As I began to learn in District Six, I must love unconditionally.

John Clark fondly described an annual tradition:

For the young people who made up the most of our band in those days, Christmas caroling held a fascination. A freezing cold night or a pea–souper fog weren't seen as excuses to cancel. "Remember when my valves froze last year?"

But tonight is a special night. "No, it's not time yet!" says our young bandmaster as he leads his charges down another street, agonizingly away from what we know will be our final destination. We have the feeling of privilege, that this gracious lady, known throughout the Army world, who chose to soldier at our little corps, will be opening her home to us and allowing us to spend an hour in her company. A few more lamp posts and we're soon outside. Almost automatically, we turn to the music of "Stars Are Shining," Colonel Skinner's melody that complements Colonel Baird's words so perfectly.

The door opens and the hall light frames the slight figure of Colonel Catherine Baird. "Do come in."

We devour hot mince pies and black currant. Then, all too soon, it's over for another year, leaving us with the fond memories that we'll tell to future generations—of those cold December nights when we "finished at Colonel Baird's."

Retirement in no way reduced Catherine Baird's ministry and influence, nor did her personal authority or prestige wane in the absence of an international position. On the contrary, both survived her departure from International Headquarters, her lengthy retirement, and even far beyond.

As would be expected, her skill and value as a writer remained as high as ever in the estimation of the company of editors. In the early summer of 1959, Brigadier Bernard Watson wrote:

Dear CB, Please do not regard yourself as "on the shelf." Your craftsmanship as a writer is not at all decrepit, any more than you are as an individual. We print stuff by young people which is not anywhere near the standard you set, and I do think you should have a try at a weekly feature; call it what you will. The eleven–plus girl is, I believe, not well catered for. I think you could do something for this age group no one else can do.

Her personal association with the renowned Commissioner Samuel Logan Brengle, great encourager and correspondent of her early officership, and the reflection in her own life of the uncomplicated holiness he preached and exemplified, made her a valued speaker at British Brengle Institutes, even in retirement. Catherine's assessment of Brengle was: "The greatest thing he did wasn't preaching or teaching, but being."

Major Phyllis Sandover, Catherine's friend and editorial colleague, discerned the secret of Catherine's own influence in a personal letter following such an Institute in June 1962:

> You brought blessing to the whole company as it is easy to discover from the conversations. Bless your heart—your hatred of cant and pretense comes like a refreshing wind to sweep away all petty prejudices which do so quickly bog us down.
>
> You little realize how much the compassionate, understanding, sane spirit of Brengle has descended on you, for the effect he had on you, you've had on some of us. I shall never cease to be grateful to God that He let me meet you, and I only pray that some small measure of the principles you hold so dear shall be seen in my life.

Such assessments neither Brengle nor Baird would have made of themselves.

Lt. Colonel and Mrs. Lawrence Jardine were officers of Balham Congress Hall from 1963 to 1966. Colonel Jardine writes of his soldier, Catherine:

> If she was in a meeting, one knew there would be power released through her presence and prayer—she never failed. I am not exaggerating when I say that always happened. Visiting the colonel in her home was always a highlight experience. Time and time again, when I was faced with difficulties and almost at my wits end, I would go to her home to spend some time with her. Sometimes the difficulties were never mentioned, but she would be so spiritually sensitive to the conversation we shared that often a chance remark, and more often her prayer, gave me the direction I needed.

They Wanted a Shepherd

They wanted a Shepherd, they said,
Dreaming of One who would
Lead them where the grass was
Bountiful, cool and green,
And the quiet waters rippled
Gently, sounding like voices speaking peace.
They were sure the new Shepherd
Would satisfy them with delectable food
To save them from the
Terrors of death, leading them at
Last to indestructible mansions.

It was such a shock
When the Shepherd came never mentioning green pastures!
His eyes were filled with compassionate love—for the lost.
And His feet shod as for a rocky road.
He scanned the crowd for some sign of His own passion
Shining in them.

Only a few of the faithful went after the Shepherd,
Stones, instead of pastures, was their lot,
And sometimes, following the lost so dear to the Shepherd,
They plunged into the deep, dark tossing waters of sorrow,
Hearing a mocking voice crying: "What about the still waters?"

But the more closely they followed the Shepherd
The more certain they were that He was leading them
To a place too black and treacherous for any save God to penetrate.
If they wanted to be with God
They must abide with the Shepherd
Seeking the lost wherever the lost might be.
Truly they were walking in the valley of the shadow of death—
Death was all around on
Every side—but God
Was smiling at death,
And when He smiled death disappeared,
Even as a mist dissolves,
Disclosing a view surpassing all finite beauty.
Fear departed, for the faithful knew now that death was neither evil nor fearful.
They understood the green pastures, still waters, protection,
And laden tables were the inner wealth
Of communion with the Eternal and known to
Those who follow the good Shepherd on His perilous journey to seek the lost,
And on their journey, are at home
Forever in the house of the Lord.

11

No Little, Narrow Places

B oth Catherine and her brother Sam had traveled extensively, with the consequent broadening of their minds and understanding. Neither had married. The great friendship they happily shared, as children in Australia and in youth in South Africa, had continued through their adult lives. While serving in the United States, Catherine had shared Sam's lovely home in Chicago.

On Sam's retirement the two single Bairds once again joined forces. Sam sold his home in Chicago to live in Balham with Catherine, in a rented apartment situated in the home of her friend Dorothy Hunt. The years they shared together in London were reminiscent of their happy childhood days.

Her friend, Dawn Dawe, recalls:

> Thinking of Colonel Baird always makes me smile. She had a delightful sense of humor. Once, in a mad moment, I agreed to have my face made up in a London store. The result was terrible, but had to be shared—a quick telephone call to Colonel Baird. "Come straight away, the kettle will be on." She opened the door, and then her arms. "Come in, my dear; this is a home for 'fallen women.'" We laughed and laughed, and she tried to persuade me not to wash it off until I'd been home.
>
> There would be her little asides occasionally in Army meetings. "I don't want a mansion in heaven. I'd rather have a cottage. I can't see myself sitting on a cloud, twanging a harp. I expect I'll be cooking cakes."

Catherine's humor spiced her writings. It permeated her personal essays, and in her published escapades of Ethelburga, the winsome wit of a fun–loving Catherine is endearing.

A friend's telephone would ring late morning. "Catherine Baird here. Can you help me out? I just happen to have baked too much this morning. There is a large apple pie [or a cake or some scones] here I could not possibly use myself. Could you possibly do me a favor and take them off my hands, please?"

Perhaps less discerning, but equally grateful, were neighbors in need, or launderette ladies undergoing hard times, surprised by caller Catherine at their door, explaining that somehow she "had happened to bake too much and wondered if they could relieve her of these."

Her friends, by long experience, weren't fooled by the "just happened to have made too much" line. But they gladly "helped her out."

Catherine's continuing participation in councils and at conferences for musicians, local officers and youth groups remains outstanding in the memories of the delegates. Her rapport with young people was quite remarkable. Heather Coutts was a student when she first met Catherine and recalls:

> She used to love to come to the Students' Fellowship weekends and talk to the students. She was a very popular visitor there. Very often she would be asked to speak on holiness, which was a subject that students were particularly interested in at the time, but it was always holiness with a very human approach. As ever there was rapt attention when the slight, softly spoken and elderly Catherine stood tranquilly at the rostrum before students and graduates, disarmed and disarming, teaching unarguable truth with words of transparent simplicity, such as: "The task of a Christian is to live as a Christian." After all, she was one of the fellowship—a colleague. Forever herself a student, and a formidably honest one, she was qualified to teach.

Even in those retired days, Catherine was still studying systematically, encouraging the continuation of classes led by Dr. England of the University of London. A letter dated February 26, 1962 from the department of extramural studies confirmed agreement to a proposed arrangement:

> Dear Miss Baird, Mr. Thomas has asked me to reply to your kind letter in which you expressed the wish of your fellow students to continue studying with Dr. England next session at the Clapham and Balham Institute. The proposal you make is entirely acceptable to us here, and both Mr. Thomas and I would like to convey our very best wishes to you and Dr. England for another successful class.

Apart from his enviable reputation at the University of London, Dr. England was remembered with affection and respect in his home town of

Bexhill–on–Sea, where from 1928 to 1971 he served as Minister of St. George's Presbyterian Church of England.

Douglas Collin, having previously led songster brigades at Tottenham Citadel, Barking and Romford corps, was already a graduate at the time of Catherine's participation in The Salvation Army Students' Fellowship annual weekends. He fondly recalls Catherine's association and repeatedly invited her to functions:

> We invited her for her aura! You could almost touch the aura! What a privilege to have come within her orbit. She was a gracious lady. When you were with her she made you feel better than you really were. I suppose my most hallowed memories were when we used to invite her to lead devotions at our Students' Fellowship weekends at Sunbury Court. Always, one was in the presence of Christ because Cathy was there. I suppose the greatest influence has been her poetry. She was a true poet—never any doggerel; often containing meaning beyond the words. An expression of the inexpressible, and yet always compelling.

Collin quotes "Breath of Eternity" as one of his favorites from Catherine's book *The Sword of God*:

I meet Him
When I'm walking down
Long avenues of thought,
In a broad Land of Silences,
Where I explore
When I feel stifled
By life's little, narrow places.

I cannot tell
The words He speaks,
What robes He wears,
Or, if His form
Be fair to look upon.
I only know,
When I return,
I have inhaled a breath
Of spaces where God is;
It cannot be subdued
By little, narrow places.

"To me," Collin comments, "that is the definitive expression of Cathy's relationship with God." As an eminent musician, he considers Lt. Colonel

Norman Bearcroft to be at top form in his composition of three Catherine Baird poems in the suite "Reflections." "In this work," he reckons, "Norman had given the Army one of its finest compositions in its choral repertoire."

If Catherine's poem "Breath of Eternity" caused Douglas Collin to ponder on the "long avenues of thought," the sentiments of a private letter to the General of the time, Wilfred Kitching, defined some of them. Dated February 1, 1958, not long after Catherine's retirement, the letter expresses the abhorrence of the idea of anyone who may "set up within our ranks a witch–hunting attitude." By her definition, "a witch–hunter is one who seeks, by any means, to suppress or even damage and slander those whose honest convictions do not coincide with his [or her] own. We cannot expect young people to forgive it in the Army where men [and women] should be occupied with more lofty pursuits."

> I have known more people to be hunted down because they were more maturely sound than the ignorant huntsman. Christian tolerance forbade retaliation and, in any case, the more mature men become, the less ignorant they are in thinking they are the only ones who can interpret truth.

The "school of thought" Catherine deplored was: "that of the closed mind—one that will not receive more light."

> Surely anyone should be ashamed to have, after 30 years, no deeper, clearer understanding of the atonement, holiness, last things, and other great doctrines, than he had at the beginning. And surely, this deeper knowledge does not mean he has departed from that he first knew. Given the alphabet, a child can write simple words and little more. In manhood, he may write a sonnet. But that does not mean he no longer believes that "cat" spells cat.
>
> The second deplorable attitude of mind is that of worshipping the written Word rather than the living Word. The godly scholars and saints who gave us the Bible in its present form never could have dreamed we would mistake them for God, or regard their work as infallible. Our Founder did not so consider them. Martin Luther said: "The Bible is the crib wherein our Lord is laid." To disregard this fact is surely a denial of the "holy writ" mentioned in your letter.
>
> As I said, I shall not trouble you further, but if we want the sort of young people who care more for truth than for privileges and places, we shall have to consider a matter of such vital importance without fear or prejudice.
>
> God be with you. Sincerely yours, Catherine Baird, Colonel.

The Students' Fellowship magazine carried and covered a variety of subjects. Frustrations were expressed and critical comments aired with articles of sound spiritual sense. One issue carried a compliment to their colleague Catherine Baird by student "Antonio," who might now admit to being Dr. John Coutts, friend and admirer of Catherine since his youth. Antonio's letter provides delightful insight into the respect and affection in which this senior student was held by the fellowship:

> Dear Sir, Us men in the YP band aint got much time for that their stoodents fellowship (snobs fraternal our Ern calls it) and we aint usually got much time for High Up officers either, all done up in purple and fine rainment as the Bible says. Which makes it odd to fine us riting an artikle in praise of our freind Catherine Beard.
>
> I must tell you she has had all kinds of adventures. Then she go to USA and live in Chicago at the same time as the notorious All Capone. She was by this time on the Army HQ ande riting a great deal hwich she still does. Also she rites poitry some of it is in the song bok, but I dont hold it against her and some of the poitry is supposed to be very good.
>
> Now one thing you have to like about this lady is the fack that she is on your level. She has a very nice kitchen in the upstairs of a big house down off the Balham Eye Road, with kind of China stuck upon the wall if you see what I mein. Now in this hear kitchen she bake bread; last time we up there we sat the yeast bubbling around as good as a science experiment a hear Algenon says. But then his dads an officer and he pass eleven plus and is a ded cert for that stoodents fellowship sonner or later. But to get back to the kitchen; I do like the cakes and tea you get which hwile refined as you'd especk with such a laidy is not polite, by polite I mein what you get in some places, tiny samwiches that would starve a tadpoll. Fair drives you up the wall.
>
> Not only do this lady give tea and cakes to the needy she also do many other good works but unlike most she do not drive you mad in the prossess. For instance she is a pillar of the over sixties club and is active collecting subscriptions and cheering the old folk. some of them are all right but some are miserable old codger. She also goes from the supreme to the ridculus by going to meetings of the stoodents fraternal wich my dad says is one step worse than the drummers [the Drummers' Fraternal—group of percussionists led by Major Burnal Webb, father of Major Joy Webb] and throws the Army aint wot it used to be. However I think this laidy of which I rite have a deep love for soals and feel sorry for some of the xrazy mixed up crowd. She is kind and freindly to the young as I already say.
>
> Well in the end she come to London and work on HQ on what I believe they call the litter department though this must be some kind of joke. She rite more books and edit *The Young Soldier* hwich is not bad as Army papers go. She dont work there no more but is very busy with all the things she has to do.

Now I have described this laidy I will stop: Poor soppy Algernon who will call her auntie caff says his dad say she is a mistick. Hwich is a dirty insult because all her freinds know she is normal and freindly. Clever Aljy say he wonders if my story have a kernel of historissity, hwotever that is; so there is two things to pay him out for next week after practise.

Well I have finish and I dont mind if you print it or not. Nor will the laidy I rite abot, I once hear her say she dont beleive in all of this hoisting of Commissionaire Brengle and suchlike before the throne of grace.

Yours with defiance contemp, and slight regard (Shake Spear)

Antonio on behalf of the Black Hand Gang. You have been warned!!!!!

In his student days (from 1957 to 1960), John Coutts lodged in Dorothy Hunt's house. His fiancée, Heather Cooper, was always a most welcome visitor there. Heather has the happiest recollections of times shared on Bushnell Road, and recalls:

A big old house—Three people living there—CB and her brother Sam, who was a very shy and gentle person, and of course Miss Hunt herself. Three elderly people, but it was always a house where there was a lot of laughter, and a great deal of practical kindness and understanding.

We'd often sit together and have a good laugh, and really, I mean a good laugh! There was one occasion when CB, Miss Hunt, John and I were sitting having a cup of tea after a meal—always well fed in that establishment. Miss Hunt was recalling an occasion when she went to a funeral. She got to the crematorium realizing that she was in fact very unsuitably dressed, because she'd got a hat with flowers on it, and so in order not to cause any embarrassment she whipped it off and left it at the door. Lo and behold, to her great horror, the coffin [passed in parade] eventually, and there was her hat on top of the coffin! As she recounted this story we all just wept with laughter, CB included.

Heather and John never forgot the most practical support of the establishment at Bushnell Road. In addition to the kind hospitality of Miss Hunt and her open house, Catherine Baird herself would go the extra mile, unobtrusively cutting through conventional Army red tape when she deemed it sensible and kind to do so.

In the Army's training college, Heather fell victim, in the company of other cadets, to a general flu epidemic. As she recalls, she was not "bouncing back" as quickly as desirable. One day, a member of the staff appeared and informed Heather that it was decided that she should have a break from the college to recuperate. This break was pursued by Catherine Baird behind the scenes. However, Catherine did not mention the fact that Heather's fiance, John Coutts, was living in her house.

Naturally, Heather was delighted with the provision—her health and spirits doubtlessly improved. This arrangement, not typical of the rigid regime of Denmark Hill at the time, showed a very human side of Catherine Baird.

The kindness, understanding and support of the Bushnell Road household was a godsend to Heather and John, who had a long engagement. John was almost twenty-six when they married. Neither Heather nor John had parents living in England as their wedding day approached. Heather's parents, Lt. Colonel and Mrs. Randolph Cooper, were in East Africa, and Commissioner and Mrs. Frederick L. Coutts were in Australia. Wedding plans and arrangements, therefore, were their own responsibility. "Both Catherine and Miss Hunt," Heather says, "kind as ever, would help in any way we desired, and were most supportive."

> I told CB a well–kept secret, that I'd planned to get married in white—a white Salvation Army uniform. [Soon they would be traveling to serve in Nigeria.] I wasn't sure quite how I was going to go about getting this "wedding dress" made.
>
> Now CB always had many many people whom she quietly visited, looked after and befriended. There was a Hungarian lady who lived not very far away. CB said: "She's most eccentric, and she keeps a whole houseful of cats, but she's very good at dressmaking. You draw the kind of dress you want, and I'm quite sure she'd make it for you." So what [I] in fact did, I drew the kind of uniform dress I wanted made. I went and bought the white cotton poplin material and we went to see this lady, CB and I, and showed her what I wanted.
>
> Apparently she didn't really use a pattern, she just "snip, snipped," and took the measurements and all the rest of it, so I kept my fingers crossed and left her to it.
>
> Then the day came to go and collect my wedding dress, and it was fine, but when I got it round to 24 Bushnell Road, CB said to me, "Is it okay?" I said "Yes, it's lovely and it fits beautifully," and I just had to grin. I said, "there's only one thing wrong. It's the cat's paws all over it!"
>
> Poor CB was absolutely horrified, because of course she'd suggested this lady make the dress and she hadn't bargained for this result! But CB was determined herself that she would wash it and she would make it fit for the great day, and indeed she did!"

"Through all the years since our wedding day," said Heather, "up until the time CB died, she never ever forgot our wedding anniversary. The one thing we could always depend on was a card, usually with a little gift enclosed, and certainly a message."

On the afternoon of February 26, 1967, a festival in honor of the works of Catherine Baird took place in the Army's Regent Hall, London. Several unpublished settings of her words were featured. Brigadier William Burrows, then editor of *The Musician*, praised her "magnificent contributions" to the Army's continuing "armory of song." Two of Colonel Baird's poems, "Love Chose a Garment" and "Requiem," were set to music and presented by then–Captain Joy Webb.

The versatility of the colonel's pen was illustrated in the songster brigade anthem, "A Song of Praise" and the young people's singing company anthem, "When You Were a Child Like Me."

The songsters and band presented a new suite—Catherine Baird's poem "God Is Our Home" set to music by songster leader Michael Babb. This piece was described in *The Musician* as "the climax of the afternoon, both distinguished and thoroughly exhilarating."

Anticipating the event, Babb observed:

> Composers like Catherine Baird's work for two very important reasons: the quality of her poetry—in rhythm, form and style, as well as its content. Her understanding of what will be effective with music is a quality that cannot be seen on cursory examination, but which is very real.

Major Joy Webb, one of the Army's premier musicians, added dramatically to the Army's vocal repertoire. Webb has no doubt that Catherine Baird has had the most profound effect on her early attempts to write poetry and song lyrics. "I have imbibed more than I can tell from her poetic spirit," Webb states.

As the years went by, Dorothy Hunt's condition worsened to the point where she needed day and night nursing care. During these years, Catherine took upon herself the enormous responsibility of caring for her completely. Miss Hunt was a well–built lady, and Catherine was small and slight. Overcome with weariness, Catherine said, "Sometimes I was so tired that when I went to the meeting, if I shut my eyes I had to open them quickly in case I went to sleep."

Well–meaning and caring friends, appalled by her incredible responsibilities, sought to dissuade Catherine from allowing herself to be "burdened and imprisoned." Mindful of her tremendous talent, they suggested she was "neglecting her stewardship."

"Yet I knew," she said, "I could do no other. I knew, too, that I was neither burdened nor imprisoned, but privileged and free." Catherine knew and declared at the time that if she had not nursed her friend, and, as the need arose, her brother Sam, she would not have been able to write.

Catherine took driving lessons and passed her test on the first try, but never drove again. Sam, who eventually stopped driving, gave her his car. Typically, Catherine gave it away.

To young Quest conference members at Sunbury Court, Catherine explained the source of her lines in "Journeying Safely."

I am very fond of animals to start with, and I kept reading that story of the Good Samaritan over and over again. I thought of how the Samaritan bound up the wounds and gave his money, but most important of all, he gave his donkey's back. And he himself, because he wanted this man he had picked up and helped to go safely home, gave the thing that was most important to him, and he took the hard way.

To me, the story is about my brother. I had a wonderful brother, and I would not have been able to look after my friend financially if he had not come over from America. He gave up a very beautiful home in America, and came over here to live so that I could journey safely.

Of course, in another way, it is very much like our Lord, who gave up everything, and took the hard way so that we could journey safely home to God. I am sure we never would have found our way to God if it hadn't been for Jesus.

That poem is really a story about one who, to me, showed the Christ spirit and in doing so, he showed me what Jesus did when He died fo us. There is the thing most precious to me, so that we can journey safely home.

Journeying Safely

His donkey had a coat of grey, shaggy and plain,
Yet soft as plush to tired limbs;
Her patient eyes were brown as earth,
And bright as new–formed pools of rain.
Meekly she bore her master's weight
O'er rugged hills and treacherous roads,
Easing his journey with her strength,
Sparing his feet the heated stones.
Perhaps she sensed the gratitude
In gentle hands that guided her,
Perhaps she halted, knowing how
Her master would not turn aside

Nor leave the wounded traveler
Bleeding and broken in the way.
Silent she waited in the sun,
Bending her head, and listening
For sounds remote from human ears.
Silent, with muscles swiftly braced,
She watched her master's offering:
He used his skills to bind and heal;
He spared his wealth to purchase care;
Most lovely gift of all, he gave
His donkey's broad and supple back,
Lifting the drooping traveler there.
And for himself, the sharpened stones,
The rising dust, the heavy load,
The abysmal weariness unknown
To any save the ones who toil
That he who cannot walk may ride
To shelter and, with strength restored,
May safely journey to his home.

After seven years of home nursing by Catherine, on December 5, 1969, Dorothy Hunt passed away. Thereafter Sam, now very frail and in need of his sister's care, would live only six weeks longer. An intelligent and thoughtful person, Sam Baird had spared no mental effort in his lifelong search for truth. His essay of sixty–eight pages, titled "Search for Truth," is a profound testimony to his own seeking.

Catherine's poem "Country Sparrow," written after Sam's death and intended for publication only after her own passing, gives witness to her faith.

Country Sparrow

He lived among the garish high–rise flats,
But dreamed of cattle on the mountain slopes
Where once he watched the new–born lambs at play
Rejoicing in the warm and friendly sun.
Beyond the boastful concrete towers he saw
The fleecy clouds move peacefully along,
Like vessels on a boundless azure sea,
Their gallant sails flung open to the breeze;
With upraised eyes he viewed ethereal heights—
"The Lord is here!" he said.

He sadly mourned decaying rubbish heaps
Where careless hands had tossed unwanted trash,

But lo! One morning on a summer day
A miracle addressed his startled sight:
A single rose, her petals blessed with dew
Poured out her fragrance o'er the dismal scene—
His aged head in reverence bowed low—
"The Lord is here!" he said.

He plied his way along the busy street,
His weary steps unsteady now, and slow,
While streams of traffic sped and, somewhere near,
A siren's screech disturbed the heated air;
He fancied he could catch the rhythmic flow
Of waters, clear as crystal, passing by
His father's cottage nestling in the glen.
"The Lord is here!" he said.

He did not feel the faint and fluttering beat
Of his fast failing heart; he only heard
A blackbird sing, a sparrow's cheerful chirp,
And wondered did the feathered creatures know
The world's Creator cared if they should fall?
How near the river seemed, how sweet the taste
Of ice–cold water pressed against his lips!
How beautiful the cool hand on his brow,
The kindly face, the softly spoken word!
There, like a happy conqueror come home,
He whispered with a last relinquished breath:
"The Lord, My Lord is here!"

The death of her dear brother Sam left Catherine, in her own words, "rather stunned." Again, she shared personally with her friends of Quest:

> I realize that everybody has to have some kind of sorrow or hardship in this world and it is a gift you can give to God. I thought, I am just pitying myself. I am not thinking of them. They are released. They have gone to God, or at least they are still with God, because it is only the body that falls away and the spirit is still with God. I am just feeling sorry for myself. I will hand this gift over to God.
>
> And I did, and when I look back at that experience in my life, which some people criticized because they said it was affecting my writing, I think it was the most wonderfully spiritually rewarding experience I have ever had in my life.
>
> It is not a thing that you talk about, but I am talking about it to you because the poem might mean something to you some day. If you have not already passed through such an experience, it will come some day.

Catherine Baird's audience that day was generally too young to have already experienced the tension of caring for a loved one in terminal illness or the turmoil of bereavement. The years may have brought to some of them the "gift" of which Catherine wrote and spoke. In that event, Catherine's testimony of her "treasure, bright with tears" may well serve as a shaft of light and guidance.

As she had cared for her friend and brother, Catherine found great comfort in other "residents" of her home—her beloved pets. As a young girl, her sister Winnie had looked at baby Catherine lying in her cradle and longed to tell her that as well as the friendly garden wildlife creatures, which were as good as family pets, there was a gray kitten in a cozy basket at the back of the woodshed where the washtubs hung. It didn't take Catherine long to continue the Baird tradition of passion for pets. Her fondness for animals knew no frustration as a child in Australia or South Africa. Her joy reached a peak when she lived on Driefontein farm, where pets, farm animals and wildlife abounded.

Now, after the trauma of bereavement and moving home (the change of accommodation from Dorothy's property to another apartment in Balham, recently vacated by Brigadier Catherine Beecham, another retired officer), Catherine's two cats, Esmeralda and Arabella, provided an oulet for her love and care and the inspiration for many a humorous article. In one parable–essay, "Esmeralda," Catherine writes:

> Sitting on her fence post listening to sounds we cannot hear, sniffing scents we cannot find, Esmeralda seems to have a thinking–box in her brain. She has never bothered about words; her whole species speaks the same language, and it's all the same to her if a Russian or a Siamese comes to visit her.
>
> Of course there are a few fights in the garden, but they are most enjoyable and no one is killed. In fact, Esmeralda's chief aim in life is to propagate and preserve the lives of her offspring.

Upon her move to the new apartment, Catherine met Arabella, a kitten she eagerly adopted from Brigadier Beecham. Arabella found a home for life, and Catherine had inherited a pet which was to live with her for many years, and predeceased her by only a few weeks.

There was nothing mediocre or small about Catherine's world. For instance, to her loving owner, Arabella the cat was more than just a pet around the house to be fed. She was a personality to be cared for.

Of her own passing, Catherine had written to a friend: "I don't think bugles will sound for me on the other side. There may be a few soft purrs from sundry cats and tail wags from dogs, or cheeps from sparrows."

REDEMPTION

Show me Thyself, O perfect Love!
My love was fashioned in the world;
It bears the marks of earth.
Art Thou above and underneath
And reaching out on either side
Beyond all measurement, all thought,
Or, art Thou as the summer morn
Whose beauty springs from stormy death
And silently relinquished life?
These are but images I see
When groping in eternity,
And, in Thy meadowlands I find,
Deep–rooted, Christ, the living Vine;
Now, humbly, willingly, I come,
In Him to join my love with Thine,
Awaiting Thy redeeming power.

12

REFLECTIONS

In 1975 members of the editorial and literary departments gathered at International Headquarters for a double celebration—to mark the eightieth birthday (October 12) of Colonel Baird, and to launch her new book of poems, *Reflections*. The literary secretary of the day was Catherine's longtime friend Commissioner Kathleen Kendrick and the editor in chief was Colonel Brindley Boon, editor of *The War Cry*.

"It was an inspiring occasion," Colonel William Clark recalls. "Colonel Baird spoke about her life, writing, and the use of words in the service of the kingdom." Of Catherine's many poems and songs which have appeared in Salvation Army publications worldwide since she began her literary career in Chicago, *Reflections* is considered her most personal work, representing the best of her extraordinary vision and talent. In his foreword to the book, General Frederick Coutts had this to say:

> The gift of insight and mastery of expression which these poems evidence need no commendation from me. With all other readers, I can only give thanks both for them and the author, for she and her work are fruits of The Salvation Army tree which continue to surprise the unknowing by their variety and delicacy.
>
> The colonel is my senior—for she was an officer of The Salvation Army before I had given that high calling even a moment's thought. She was the editor, and held the appointment for nine years of *The Young Soldier* before ever I set foot inside International Headquarters. Later, for good measure, she took over the editorship of the Army's world youth magazine as well, and ended her official active service as literary secretary to the General.
>
> Yet this is the third volume of her poems to be published. Here is the rare possession of a creative mind which could also meet the unforgiving deadlines of press days. She may look slight in body, but showed herself possessed

of an inner strength which enabled her to continue to live in the top flat of a three–storied Victorian house in a south–west London suburb through the daily hazards of the blitz. She is now 80 years of age, but her mind remains alert and questioning; her heart is as outgoing as ever; and, as these pages bear witness, her spirit is still open to those divine intimations which testify to the reality of things unseen.

Those into whose hands this collection of sixty poems may come will realize to whom the "Lines to a Writer" could be addressed. To the author herself!

Lt. Colonel Lily Sampson, for years a colleague and friend of Catherine Baird, observed that Catherine's biography may be found in her poetry. *Reflections* is certainly autobiographical.

Throughout all of *Reflections* we are allowed glimpses of events and personalities of particular significance in Catherine Baird's life. Her willingness to leave home on the Driefontein Farm which she loved, to respond to the need which she felt was the call to Salvation Army officership, doubtless influenced also by the commitment of her sister Winnie and brother–in–law Walter, is echoed in her song "The Call of God." We learn of the life–changing encounter of "The New Lieutenant" with the evils of District Six in South Africa.

In "Redemption," which opens with Catherine's prime prayer, "Show me Thyself, O Perfect Love!" we may accompany her in the most brilliantly described experiences and journeys of her heart and mind when "groping in eternity" and share "the search that began with earliest officership."

"God's Reckless Son" portrays the cost of taking one's stand on pacifism, of which principle Catherine Baird was convinced. "Going Away and Coming Back" tells of Catherine's longing to escape, though temporarily, from the "heated walls of the city, the clanging telephones, the screeching traffic" to a spiritual retreat, from which she would return refreshed to the rushing world, the clatter, and the jeering throng, to repay "Him who loves me." "This Is the Fellowship" shows how Catherine felt at one with the everyday people she met in the riverside cafe during the blitz of the Second World War—"We shared the common perplexities and a deep and terrible yearning for a better world."

Catherine's deep admiration of Carvosso Gauntlett, in his utter self–giving, is the source of "Calling More Fools." Her great love of children, in whose service she had invested most of her active–officership years, is apparent in "Dreaming" and "Across the Street."

"A King in the Band" records her appreciation of the many Salvationist–bandsmen "whose work behind the scenes is an act of worship even greater than their most perfect musical performance." The captain and other characters in Catherine's retirement corps of Balham are described in "They Wanted a Shepherd."

Catherine's original and stark "One Word for Judas," whose "paths are too dangerous for me, too dark and terrifying" for "only the Lord of light dare tread the treacherous realms where demons rave," displays her courage and divine perception in handling and understanding Scriptural records.

The title poem "Reflections" is a beautiful tribute to and description of her brother Sam. "The Gift" poignantly portrays Catherine's great grief at Sam's death. His generosity of spirit she compares with the Good Samaritan and even Jesus in "Journeying Safely."

Despite its difficulties and distresses, Catherine made no secret of her love of human life and the present lovely world, and her honest reluctance to surrender it. This is confessed in her song "Brief Is Our Journey," where the prospect of physical death is made tolerable only by her commitment to love and her implicit trust in Jesus, and everlasting life. Her lines "Home to Thee" are Catherine's prayer that when her wonderful human life span is at an end, her soul's journey to God may be soft and silent. It was so.

Reflections is a beautiful, honest, and profound book—a legacy to enrich readers beyond measure. The reader feels that she too, as in Catherine's final poem in the volume, has broken an alabaster box, and the fragrance of the priceless ointment is spilled, for us, "like perfumed breezes from the seas of God."

Alabaster Box

Broken the alabaster box;
The priceless spikenard spilled
O'er ages, and the rarest scent
Poured out upon eternity!
O enemy, who struck the shattering blow,
Now shalt thou never more escape
This fragrance. Everywhere
Like perfumed breezes from the seas of God
'Twill meet thy senses;
Thou must breathe or die!

Catherine Baird's efforts in the practical support of her corps officers could be as varied as their needs. In 1978, in Catherine's eighty–third year,

Major Charles and Mrs. Sheila Groom were appointed to the command of the Balham corps. Sheila Groom's mother, Mrs. Elizabeth E. Reynolds, who was suffering from cancer, came to live with them. To allow Sheila to participate as much as possible in corps activities, Catherine would sit in with Mrs. Reynolds regularly on Sunday evenings. Sheila remembers:

> Colonel helped me to nurse my mother by sitting with her regularly so that I could go to the meetings, and making delicacies like egg custards to tempt her appetite. I don't know how many word search puzzles they did between them, but whenever I look at a word search I think of them both.

For many years Mrs. Reynolds had liked a cigarette, and actually "rolled her own," though the tobacco content in the paper was so small the family used to joke that it was a substitute for a child's "comforter." Her daughter continues:

> Towards the end of her life Mother was becoming too weak for the effort of rolling the cigarettes. Colonel was concerned that when she was sitting with her Mum might not be able to "roll her own" cigarette and would be uncomfortable as a result. So Colonel Baird insisted on being taught how to do the job!

Trained though she now was, Catherine never needed to put her new skill into practice, for Sheila observes:

> I think the idea of Colonel rolling her cigarettes was too much for Mum, and she gave up smoking for the last few months of her life. Perhaps it was a measure of their friendship that each was so concerned about the other.

Although he had known Colonel Catherine Baird by repute and on "nodding acquaintance" for years, it was on his first "official" encounter with Catherine that the then Major Norman Bearcroft, national bandmaster for the British territory, discovered her singleness of mind when it came to a timely test of priorities. Bearcroft recalls his surprise then and admiration of Catherine Baird:

> The first connection I ever had with her was when she was asked if she would write the song of dedication for the commissioning of the cadets in 1967. She said she would if I would write the music. I said I would be very glad. I wrote the music (ultimately the song was published as "My Solemn Vow") and took it round to her home.
> "Oh, I'm so pleased to see you," she said. "It isn't very often people come and see me with music." I went in and we sat and talked.

When it came time to leave, I said, "Well, Colonel, I'll see you on the Friday, then, at the Royal Albert Hall."

"Oh, no; I won't be there."

"You won't be there? You'll miss your song!"

"No," she said; "Friday's the day I take Mrs. Williams out in her wheelchair."

Then I said a silly thing; I realized what a foolish thing it was to say. I said, "Couldn't you change the day for Mrs. Williams?"

"No," she said, "I couldn't change the day for Mrs. Williams."

And there I am, thinking, the Albert Hall, with everyone there; and the spotlight and everything. But for this woman, taking Mrs. Williams out in the chair was more important. That's when I realized what kind of a person she was.

Colonel Baird always found it difficult to understand why Salvation Army groups, music leaders among them, valued so highly the occasions when she was their special guest in conference. Jill Bearcroft, involved as she always was in such gatherings planned and led by her husband, Lt. Colonel Norman Bearcroft, cherishes a memorable moment with visitor Catherine to a songster leaders' conference at Sunbury Court. The Army's conference center, a charming Georgian mansion set in its own spacious grounds, stands in Sunbury–on–Thames, virtually across the road from the Thames River. Once through the entrance, the visitor follows a winding drive leading through the gardens to the house door. Jill recalls:

I was waiting by the front door for Colonel Baird to arrive, and when the car drew up I went down the steps to greet her. She caught hold of my arm and we went up the steps together. I opened the front door, and as she went in she caught hold of my arm—very tightly—and stood there quietly, so I stood very quietly beside her. Then she turned to me and said: "I know you can feel it too—all the prayers of good people coming out of the walls and surrounding us."

Corps sergeant–major Eric Burn of Bedlington, England has captured on tape the content of Catherine Baird's visit to such a conference of songster leaders at Sunbury in the summer of 1981. Burn remembered: "The setting was just right—the main lounge of Sunbury Court; the comfortable armchairs; the light glistening on the marvelous chandelier; an attentive and sympathetic audience creating a perfectly relaxed atmosphere.

"Commissioner Kathleen Kendrick spoke on the theme 'Glimpses of Glory' and to a person we felt we shared just that. She set the scene for a "once–

in–a–lifetime" experience. Major Norman Bearcroft introduced Colonel Catherine Baird in glowing, indeed loving terms.

"The colonel appeared as a frail, silver–haired, elderly officer, as 'one of the saints of God.' Her obvious nervousness was apparent in her mannerism, her gentle protests at the major's complimentary introduction, the slight shake in her voice, all belied the might of the Spirit to be revealed as the interview progressed:

N.B.: When did you start writing?

C.B.: My mother was five feet in height and very small in stature. She had been a school teacher and had never done any work with her hands. By the time I was eleven years old she was an officer with five children. Her hands were no longer soft and I wrote my first poem about "marked, lined, veined hands." It wasn't so very marvelous. I took the poem to school with me. At that time, I was in a class of boys. Someone got hold of it, and it was read aloud to the whole class. I nearly died with embarrassment.

N.B.: I know how very difficult it is sometimes to commence any form of artistic work. Can you tell us how you get words flowing?

C.B.: My inspiration is born within. The thoughts commence inside and they would perish and die if I didn't get them down. I believe God wants me to do it and so I set them down. When this is done, however, I invariably feel dissatisfied. I have to seek to improve the words I have used to convey the feelings of my heart.

N.B.: Isn't it correct that while in America you collaborated with Emil Soderstrom on the production of songs?

C.B.: That's right. He was a most unusual character, very humble and yet a masterful musician. He wrote his first music at the age of nine. It was because of Emil Soderstrom that I first had something published in England.

N.B.: We have just heard Captain Diane Lillicrap [now Major Diane O'Brien] sing that very beautiful song, "When Jesus Looked O'er Galilee." Will you talk to us about that song?

C.B.: A young woman had just suffered the very worst kind of sorrow and had written some music. I was given this music and took it home. I played it over and over again on the piano. The music spoke very clearly to me. It was a truly spiritual experience—just as listening to Beethoven can be a spiritual experience. As I played the music over and over again I began to think of Jesus as a young boy, of His being in the Temple and first realizing His destiny. Of how, having done this, He had to return home to His parents and be subject to their authority. It seems to me such a greater thing He did, when you consider He knew what He had to go through, just what He had to do, and yet He went ahead and did it.

I love the sea. I've seen the moon pick up water and drop it on people's hair. The last verse, I suppose, reflects my love of the wind. I recall as a girl running over the veld in Africa, with the warm wind in my hair and feeling truly free. I believe Jesus must have known that He would overcome and, like the end of another of my songs, I am sure He didn't say, "I will overcome," but rather said, "I have overcome."

N.B.: Can I ask you to talk to us about your song "O Love Revealed on Earth in Christ?" It's a favorite of mine and somehow I've never felt the tunes available for it truly do the poetry justice.

C.B.: O Yes! It's a song of love. It amounts to the climax of the story I told about myself and my times in District Six in Africa. It shows the development within myself of the knowledge and understanding of the love of God for mankind whatever their state. I asked myself the question, "How can I find out about a God of such love and compassion?" Jesus, of course, is the answer.

I wrote the song during the war. At that time, I suffered great inner conflict but eventually came to the conclusion that the only answer was love, that with love within me the events of this life were of little consequence. It is only important that the love of Jesus is within me. I realized that I must find out how to love people unconditionally.

At this time a wonderful thing happened to me. I had another of those flashes of light we've talked of. It related to my understanding of the doctrine of holiness. It had troubled me for some time. I preached about it as something separate. I suppose I was trying to fit it into a pigeon hole. This really is what the last verse and chorus are about. It asks the question, "Have you got some intolerable load? Are you troubled at heart or in mind? I have cast all my weakness upon God."

N.B.: Can I ask you a little about the mechanics of songwriting, for it does not simply amount to waking up in the middle of the night with some incredible inspiration.

C.B.: Yes, you are right. It's not just inspiration. As far as I'm concerned there are two parts to my writings: (1) the inner form, (2) the outer form.

The inner form is what you may call inspiration. The outer form is what makes a poem. I believe that it comes through me and not of me, or out of me. I believe God gave me the talent and I believe that He speaks through me. I don't want to express myself. I want to express God.

The outer form is a question of discipline, of conscientiously working at the task in hand. Life is a discipline, from beginning to end.

N.B.: You say, Colonel, that you consider that the words you pen are of divine inspiration. Do you have to enquire after such inspiration? Do you have to search for it or does it burst upon your thoughts?

C.B.: The inspiration seems to come from out of the blue. It's part of the miracle of life, I suppose. I may be doing quite ordinary things and then find wonderful inspiration.

N.B.: Do you keep a notebook beside you at all times and note thoughts and inspiration you have?

C.B.: I don't keep a notebook, but if I have a special thought at night time I write it down so that it is there for the morning. Sometimes, the following morning, I have to search for the inspiration from the night before, and that's sometimes quite difficult.

N.B.: Do the answers come to you while you're walking around?

C.B.: No. Sometimes they come in the middle of an Army meeting. I don't suppose they should really, if I am paying proper attention! I can tell you that the song "O Love Revealed" came to me in the middle of a meeting at Regent Hall.

My thoughts don't always come at convenient times; not always when I'm quiet at heart. They have sometimes come when I've been very angry. I generally put my ideas down at once and polish them later. One idea suggests another and I have to be very careful. Instead of finding a river I find tributaries off the tributaries. This can be very trying and causes me to exercise real discipline. I find early morning is the best time to get rid of those extraneous thoughts that would sometimes sidetrack me.

N.B.: Sometimes I know composers, and indeed poets, are requested to write for some special occasion or special theme. Do you mind doing this?

C.B.: I can't do it for tomorrow morning! If I'm asked to do a particular work I always ask how much time I've got. Sometimes I can write more quickly than I first anticipate. I was asked by the General to write a song for the centenary celebrations in 1965, and I considered that a great honor. I wrote the song, "A Song of Praise." There were problems surrounding the writing of that song inasmuch as time was at a premium and at that time I was nursing a sick friend and my brother was dying. Quite honestly, I wondered if I could write at all. I knew that if I was to write then it would have to be God speaking through me.

In that song I did try to express the thought that the Army should not depart from its first vision. It would be easy to forget the great love for the people so fundamental to our organization. We must keep that vision. People talk of progress, or getting on. I don't know what they mean. All that matters is that we have spiritual progress, that we are getting on inside. In writing the song I wanted the listener to feel the truth of our dedication—the reality of our vision.

> *Eternal God, our song we raise*
> *In thankful, overflowing praise,*
> *For men of faith whose power was Thine,*
> *Whose love no barrier could confine;*

They humbly offered Christ their bread,
And lo, the multitudes were fed!
Our cheerful banners are unfurled,
For Christ has overcome the world.

[Major Les Condon composed the music used for this song at The Salvation Army's Centenary event at the Royal Albert Hall in London. It was published in the *Musical Salvationist* that year, and later in The Salvation Army *Song Book*.]

C.B.: I am often overtaken by inspiration and when that happens I forget all else that is around me. But when it comes to writing to order then it's a question of breaking into inspiration, and I can't often do that. Sometimes at a certain stage in my writing I feel as if I will never get the particular work finished. The inspiration is gone. When that happens I normally leave that particular work for a few weeks and then return to it. Sometimes I have to discard it.

I've written a poem recently. I felt compelled to do so. When you reach my age you really don't know about the future. When I have such feelings as this then I can't be bothered with anything else at all. The milkman has to wait for his money, and even the cat has to wait for her milk!

N.B.: Colonel, can I ask you quite simply how you have cultivated this wisdom of when to stop?

C.B.: Discipline tells one when to stop. Sometimes I automatically stop. When one is talking of such stupendous things as the love of God it is so easy to run out of words. I feel such a weak vessel compared with the ocean of His love. My poetry must have a true economy of words. I am very aware that it is not as good as it should be. I constantly feel so weak and inadequate and yet God is so kind and understanding. He has always been willing to use the humble things in life. He has always taken loaves and fishes and used them in marvelous ways. He's taken my loaves and fishes too.

N.B.: Can I ask you about your song "Brief Is Our Journey Through the Years"?

C.B.: I love, absolutely love life. I can't bear those songs about "sweeping through the gates." I'd much rather walk through my little garden gate, thank you very much! I love this world and the people in it. I'm thinking about the beauties of nature, of my lovely friends. It is of great comfort to know that as this world ends, even more beautiful things are in store for we who love Jesus.

Bold enough to claim that the themes of her writing were directly God–given to her in the first place, Catherine Baird was still wise enough to study and acquire all possible skills of her trade—even to continuing university studies—even in her advanced age, exercising the discipline and occasional drudgery needed to perfect her work.

Catherine could see the true greatness and worth in her work—even the divinity of it—without sensing any particular greatness in herself. She even suggested on one occasion that she needed to write for God more than He needed her to write for Him.

But notwithstanding the widespread recognition of Catherine Baird's literary output, the worldwide use of her songs, and the great esteem in which she was held inside and out of The Salvation Army, in the last few years of her life she found herself occasionally dismayed by doubts as to her own worth. The mutual respect and trust between Catherine, Sidney and Jean Gauntlett allowed at that time for a helpful and needful exchange of confidences that gave Catherine a chance to express her feelings.

Jean Gauntlett, who had only known Catherine Baird since her marriage into the family in 1978, remembers the onset of Catherine's misgivings. "She often used to say, 'I feel I've done nothing with my life,' and 'I don't know what I've accomplished.' I think it's a normal thing in aging," says Jean. "We used to tell her if we used one of her songs, or if I had written one line of one of her songs, I would feel I'd done something."

Catherine Baird's greatest interest and values lay in the diligent discharge of the work to which she had been called and privileged to do, wherever and whenever she had been called, and in the love she gave to and received from so many while doing so. And when the years of nursing her friend Dorothy Hunt and her brother Sam took priority over literature and songwriting, she rightly regarded that service and her other friendships as paramount at the time.

In her advancing years, Catherine was increasingly hindered by cataracts in both of her eyes. Reading, writing, cooking, knitting and other activities which she so enjoyed were proving increasingly difficult.

When she was eighty–six, Sidney Gauntlett drove Catherine to a hospital in East London where she had two operations to remove the cataracts and have lens implants. Both operations were successful. Speaking to Sidney soon after she was released from the hospital, Catherine exclaimed: "You know, there are two things I've discovered since I had my operation. The first is how ugly I am; and the second is how dirty my house is!" This she said with a twinkle in her eye.

Of course Catherine was not ugly. "In the physical sense," observed Sidney Gauntlett, "she was not beautiful looking, but she had a beautiful face that shone from the lovely spirit within. She had a certain glow."

O Love Revealed

O Love, revealed on earth in Christ,
In blindness once I sacrificed
Thy gifts for dross; I could not see,
But Jesus brings me sight of Thee.

I come to Thee with quiet mind,
Thyself to know, Thy will to find;
In Jesus' steps my steps must be,
I follow Him to follow Thee.

O Love, invisible before,
I see Thee now, desire Thee more;
When Jesus speaks Thy word is clear;
I search His face and find Thee near.

O Love, forever claim my eyes!
Thy beauty be my chosen prize;
I cast my load on timeless grace
That my free soul may run the race.

13

Home to Thee

At ten o'clock on Good Friday morning, 1984, hundreds of Christians of the various traditions had assembled outside The Salvation Army Congress Hall in Balham for their annual procession of witness. In the crowd were several Salvationists, some of them regular participants. Among them was eighty–eight–year–old Colonel Catherine Baird—a veteran of the event.

Discussing the occasion previously, her friends Sidney and Jean Gauntlett, anxious about her strength, had advised Catherine against taking part this year, but with no success. "You're not going on this march, are you?" "Oh, yes, yes!" "Well, don't go the whole way."

Others concerned included her Salvationist friend Dawn Dawe, who had also tried to dissuade her. Dawn still remembers Catherine's response. In the quiet tone which allowed no argument, she had answered: "My dear, I may never do it again." She went, as usual, and in the unsettled weather of that day, completed all of the three mile route.

At the head of the procession, a heavy cross of wood was borne by two men. Silently the Christians walked, stopping at nine points for five minutes of worship and witness. There they prayed, heard a message and sang hymns. The procession ended with a final act of worship outside the Church of St. Boniface. Talking it over afterward with Sidney and Jean, Catherine said she had "made the grade."

"How did it go?" Sidney asked.

"Well," she said, "people didn't take any notice of us! I just had the feeling that I wish they'd pick up some bricks and throw them at us!"

"And then," thought Sidney, "I saw this frail old lady, wanting bricks to be thrown at her, and I thought of her song: 'We're in God's Army and We Fight!'"

Catherine Baird's mind remained active as long as she lived. Even so, as time went on, Sidney, Jean and others felt concerned for her continued well–being. Unsure of their own future movements, they wondered what was going to happen to Aunt Catherine if at any time she would not be able to cope.

But Catherine dismissed any suggestion that it might be wise to make some arrangement for possible residence in a Salvation Army eventide home. "We saw evidence of a slackening off a bit," noted Sidney. "We once or twice broached the subject and that was one of the few occasions when her eyes really flashed with anger. There was something in her that just rejected it out of hand and she would say, 'I'm not going to be any trouble to anybody.'"

"You can't always be sure, Auntie Catherine."

"I know! God has told me!"

"We used to talk about her 'hot line'!" Jean said with a laugh.

When the Gauntletts told her that they were going to Zambia for four months, she seemed shaken by it, and went very quiet. Understandably, to an eighty–eight–year–old, four months ahead must be viewed with some uncertainty. Apart from his medical expertise, Sidney was clearly a kindred spirit and meant a great deal to Catherine. She felt safe when he was around.

As they left, Catherine, as always, waved goodbye from her front door. "We've made her very sad," said Jean as they drove away.

Shortly thereafter, on April 28, 1984, two days before the Gauntletts left for Zambia, Catherine died.

"What immediately came to our mind," said Sidney, "when we heard that ... she had died in the hospital was: 'The Lord has told me! I'll be no trouble to anybody!'"

For some reason, possibly because of the Irish accent of her neighbor Patrick Kelly, who had found the colonel unconscious and given her name to the ambulance crew, Catherine's surname had been registered mistakenly as "Bird." This name now appeared on the hospital bed card. Her new name would certainly have amused, and even pleased, Catherine. Her strong affinity with her feathered friends was well known. Many years before, Catherine had prayed that when the time came for her to journey home, she would go silently—and that prayer had been so perfectly and gently honored.

> Lord, on a quiet sea,
> Let me sail home to Thee.

One day before the end of Catherine Baird's life, Heather Coutts felt impelled to visit her.

"We popped in. We hadn't let her know we were coming. As ever, she made a cup of tea. While she was out in the kitchen, I sat at the piano, I simply sat down and played 'Love Divine' (Catherine's favorite hymn), to the tune of Blaenwern. I played it about twice, and she came in and stood behind me, with her hands on my shoulders, and started singing the last verse:

Finish then Thy new creation,
Pure and spotless let us be;
Let us see Thy great salvation,
Perfectly restored in Thee.
Changed from glory into glory,
Till in Heaven we take our place,
Till we cast our crowns before Thee,
Lost in wonder, love and praise.

"Ever since, those words have been so very memorable. As I reversed the car to drive away," John says, "I saw a shadow of sadness fall across her face. She stood at the gate and waved goodbye, and we didn't see her again. A few days later she'd gone to heaven."

It was early afternoon on May 8, 1984. The four friends of Catherine Baird who left her home in the single official car en route to her funeral service at Balham Congress Hall were as an epitome of her life and service. General and Mrs. Frederick Coutts could be said to have represented the influential leadership of the Army, of which Catherine Baird was certainly an item. Before her retirement, Catherine had reached the most influential literary post in the worldwide Army. The General had enjoyed many years of literary association with her. He was a writer of distinction; she, through her "pen of flame," had influenced countless folk in every corner of the world.

Also in the car was Lt. Colonel Margit Gauntlett, whose family were to Catherine Baird as her own. Since childhood, to Margit, Catherine Baird had been "Auntie Cath."

The other traveler was Colonel Baird's Irish neighbor of many years, Patrick Kelly. Catherine had been Patrick's mainstay throughout, even in his occasional "less than sober" days. Patrick would deliver Catherine's newspaper and tend her garden. She had entrusted him with her keys. How he loved her. "I've lost me best friend!" he exclaimed to Margit. Today, Catherine would have been proud of him. He was immaculate—though a little "forti-fied for the occasion."

Patrick represented the enormous company of Balham neighbors and associates as dear to Catherine's heart as any of her Salvationist colleagues. They attended her funeral service in large number, and no doubt were taken rather by surprise to see such a turnout of Salvation Army personnel. They had come to pay their respect to their friend, and found themselves, to their surprise, at the funeral of a celebrity! "A little unknown lady" at the funeral service said: "We didn't know she was a colonel. We didn't know she was a poet. We only knew she was our Miss Baird and we loved her."

The spacious Belham Hall was full with Salvationists of all ranks and titles, church acquaintances, a cross–section of all cultures and classes from nearby and afar. With his customary courtesy, to the commanding officer General Coutts said, "After you, Lieutenant." The General was as much in support as in command.

Commissioner Kathleen Kendrick spoke of Colonel Baird as "a beloved friend but also as a very distinguished Salvationist." In a further tribute published in *The War Cry*, she said, "We have lost a rare spirit."

General Frederick Coutts, who brought the meditation at the service, included in his eulogy:

> All I am doing this afternoon is to speak as one of her comrade officers who was junior in years, in length of service, and in the craft we practiced in the service of God and the Army. Though our appointments were always independent, we worked with similar tools for eighteen consecutive years, during which time I learnt from her industry, I profited from her generosity, I benefited from her encouragement.
>
> One of the first tasks on which Colonel and I found ourselves working together was the proofreading of the present song book in the fifties. We were two of a quartet charged to see this through to publication. Suppose, for easy arithmetic, there are a thousand songs. This equals more than half a million letters. Half a million easy opportunities to make a mistake. I learnt from her industry.
>
> I profited by her generosity—in particular, her generosity of judgment upon people and events, especially her fellow Salvationists and Salvation Army events. She was to be found any place on the line of march where anyone was in danger of falling out. I benefited from her encouragement—but I was only one in a company whose name was legion and who were frequently young in years. Her understanding of the essentials of the Christian faith, along with her loyalty to the principles of the Army, carried her lively hearers

with her. All the same she never pulled her punches—if so inelegant a figure of speech can be applied to so gentle a lady.

She was a proclaimer—by example and word of the Christian gospel—and in this has left us an example to follow.

General Coutts, at the Memorial Service in Balham Congress Hall that evening, read the verses of Catherine's prayer–poem, "Home to Thee":

I would go silently
Lord, when I come to Thee;

Glide as some gallant barque
Into the mighty dark.

Softly and gently ride
O'er the receding tide;

Steer from the shores of time
T'ward an eternal clime.
Lord, on a quiet sea
Let me sail home to Thee.

In tribute, Catherine's poem "Home to Thee," was set to music by Lt. Colonel Norman Bearcroft. Preceded by her poems "The Christ Child" and "The Seers," the suite, titled *Reflections*, was published in January 1986.

"My most magic moment in music," said Bearcroft, "was at the Songster Leaders' Councils Festival in June 1985." In the Royal Albert Hall he was conducting the international staff songsters in the suite "Reflections." As they sang "Home to Thee," the lighting engineer, so aware of a spirit of peace, of his own volition slowly dimmed the house lights as the music of Catherine's prayer drew to a close, with: "Lord, on a quiet sea/Let me sail home to Thee." Bearcroft has since composed an arrangement of "Reflections" for brass, published in the Army's Brass Journal Festival Series, September 1999.

"Colonel Catherine Baird left a rich legacy," declared the American *War Cry*, "a prolific, powerful author, who conveyed profound truth and deep insight, editor, author, poet, spiritual guide and compassionate friend."

Monday, April 30, dawned dismally for some customers of the Chestnut Grove launderette, developed devastatingly as one by one they arrived, aghast to learn the news. Cathy Baird had died on Saturday. Her grief–stricken friends pieced together accounts of Saturday's events, impossible, it seemed, to accept, but inescapably true. Their joyous friend of many years, caring and concerned always for all of them and their families, who had turned a weekly chore into a fine fellowship, was dead. For some aged and infirm of the launderette and around the neighborhood, Catherine had been the only light in their dark and weary journey, a veritable lifeline, now suddenly broken. What would they do without her?

Salvationists may have been compensated somewhat for the death of Catherine Baird by her songs and other literary works. The launderette ladies and Balham neighbors knew nothing of her fine poetry or writings, nor of her rank or position. They only knew of her real concern for them, of her joyful visits to the launderette and to some of their homes, of her kindnesses and sharing of their lives over many years.

Two of their number happened to sit beside Lt. Colonel Norman Bearcroft at the funeral service. He was quite taken aback when one of them, in a real Cockney accent, asked, "Did you know Cathy?" They then told him how good she had been to them when things were difficult with their husbands out of work, of her visits to their homes when "by chance" she had "just happened" to have baked too many cakes, or pies, and wondered if they could "do her the favor of taking them off her hands!" Of all the London launderettes, Chestnut Grove was surely special. Cathy remained loved by the old "fellowship," in whose hearts and minds the seeds of love she had sown blossomed and continued to flower.

Next to the Army's Congress Hall in Balham there now stands Catherine Baird House. A Salvation Army Housing Association project, this four–story building was opened in 1987 by General Eva Burrows and contains twenty–four self–contained flats with living rooms, bathrooms, double and single bedrooms, including two which are fully wheelchair accessible. Occupants may live as privately as they wish, taking advantage of communal facilities such as the sitting room, laundry area, and the support of the resident warden. With her rejection of the traditional "eventide home" with its full care, such a living arrangement would have suited the independent Catherine.

As part of the corps centenary celebrations in 1991, Balham Congress Hall corps released a thirty–two–page booklet titled *Our Colonel*, produced, they said, "because so many of us loved Colonel Catherine Baird." Contributors included ladies of the launderette as well as leaders from International Headquarters, corps comrades, commanding officers past and present, recording appreciative memories of Catherine Baird, lessons learned from her, deeds done by her, and encouragement received from her. As with St. John's Gospel, there was so much more that could have been written.

Brief Is Our Journey

Brief is our journey through the years,
And fleeting are our longest days;
We cherish every laden hour
And linger o'er familiar ways;
For toil and grief, or joy and gain,
When blessed by God, are sanctified,
And friendships forged through serving Him,
With each new test, are purified.

Yet know we that the sun must set,
The darkness of the night draws near
When we, as all men, must obey
The voice inaudible, but clear,
That calls us from beyond the years,
Away from all we feel and see;
How shall we bear a last farewell,
O beauteous world, how part from thee?

With Jesus' name upon their lips,
The vale of death His servants tread;
In Him they dared believe; in Him
They dare depart; nor sigh, nor dread;
To love committing all their loves,
All counted good through peace or strife,
Content to die believing still
In Jesus, everlasting life.

APPENDIX I

Songs by Catherine Baird
In The Salvation Army *Song Book*

TITLE AND NUMBER

A Boy Was Born in Bethlehem—855
Brief Is Our Journey Through the Years—874
Eternal God, Our Song We Raise—5
Jesus, Lead Me Up the Mountain—429 (verse 3)
Jesus, Lord, We Come to Hail Thee—595
Let Thy Heart Be at Rest—739
Never Fades the Name of Jesus (translation)—63
O Bright Eternal One—36
O Father, Friend of all Mankind—796
O Love, Revealed on Earth in Christ—449
Spirit of God, Thou Art the Bread of Heaven—631
We're in God's Army and We Fight—705
What Wondrous Gifts Are in My Care—871
When Jesus Looked O'er Galilee—103

APPENDIX II

OTHER SONGS

(excluding those in The Salvation Army *Song Book*)

TITLE, COMPOSER, *MUSICAL SALVATIONIST* EDITION

Beautiful Canaan, Emil Soderstrom, November 1927
Spotless Lamb, Emil Soderstrom, February 1928
Breathe Upon Me, Emil Soderstrom, July 1928
Oh, Be Our Guest, William Broughton, June 1930
My Christ, Emil Soderstrom, August 1931
By Faith Made Strong, William Broughton, October 1932
Patriots of Love, Emil Soderstrom, October 1933
Inheritance, Emil Soderstrom, August 1934
In Love He Calls, William Broughton, September 1934
One Day, Frederick Link, May 1935
Oh, Praise the King!, Emil Soderstrom, October 1936
The Balm of Calvary, Emil Soderstrom, March 1937
My Heaven, Emil Soderstrom, October 1937
The Pilot of Galilee, Emil Soderstrom, November 1937
Come Into Thy Presence, Stephen Glover, March 1938
I Have a Friend, Emil Soderstrom, November 1938
The Pathway to Glory, D. E. Norris, January 1941
O Matchless Name, Emil Soderstrom, February 1941
Stars Are Shining, Charles Skinner, November 1941
Dedication, Bramwell Coles, November 1949
Bright Flame, Michael Kenyon, January 1950
O Light of Heaven, Bramwell Coles, March 1950
A Child Shall Bring Joy, Brindley Boon, September 1950

Love Shall Cleanse Thee, Bramwell Coles, March 1951
Angels' Song of Peace, Bramwell Coles, September 1951
Ambassadors, Bramwell Coles, January 1952
Surrender, W. F. Palstra, July 1953
Spring in Winter, Bramwell Coles, November 1953
Jesus Clearly Calls, Bernard Smith, July/August 1954
The Soul–Winners, Ray Steadman–Allen, November/December 1955
O Wind!, Michael Kenyon, January/February 1959
God Speaks, Eric Ball, January 1962
Communion Through, B. Langworthy, July 1964
A Song of Praise, Leslie Condon, July 1965
The Bread of Heaven, Edgar Grinsted, October 1966
My Solemn Vow, Norman Bearcroft, April 1979
The Sacred Gift, Peter Ayling, July 1982
O Love Revealed, Malcolm Bale, April 1983
Contemplation, Peter Ayling, January 1984
The Excellent Way, Diane Berry, January 1985
Reflections, Norman Bearcroft, January 1986
Never Fades the Name, Clifford Matthews, January 1987
In Jesus' Steps, Norman Bearcroft, January 1991
New Born, Derick Kane, July 1993
Wondrous Gifts, Rosemary S. Allen, October 1993

PUBLISHED IN *THE YOUTH SUPPLEMENT*

Jesus Is All This to Me, A. Trevelyan (English air), July 1936
Shod With Salvation, R. Nuttall, October 1936
A Child's Carol, Emil Soderstrom, November 1936
Leader of Children, Emil Soderstrom, April 1938
When Jesus Walked by Galilee, Bramwell Coles, September 1938
Fair Youth, Amid Temple's Hush, Emil Soderstrom, December 1940
Little Pilgrims, Emil Soderstrom, *Gems for Young People* No. 2
His Little Child, Emil Soderstrom, 1938
Love Is Strong Enough, Edgar Grinsted, 1942
Lord of Heaven, T. Jackson, 1953
A Boy Was Born, Diane Berry, 1975

PUBLISHED IN *NEW SONGS FOR YOUNG PEOPLE*

Our Army, Bramwell Coles, January 1950
Palaces, Michael Babb, May 1950
A Prayer, Michael Kenyon, May 1951
It Is the Lord, Michael Kenyon, January 1955
Good News, Michael Kenyon, January 1957
When Jesus Looked O'er Galilee, Ernest Fewster, January 1959
Joyful Song, Bramwell Coles, January 1961
When You Were a Child Like Me, Eric Ball, May 1962
Galilee, Lawrence Berris, January 1969

SONGS FOR HOME LEAGUE SINGERS

Let Thy Heart Be at Rest, Brahms, April 1957
House on The Rock, Diane Berry, September 1983

ABOUT THE AUTHORS

Major John C. Izzard, born in Glasgow, Scotland, became an officer of The Salvation Army in 1947 after a term of enlistment in the United Kingdom's Royal Air Force. After serving in corps appointments and then at International Headquarters and as a UK national youth crusader, he was appointed to several youth leadership positions within the United Kingdom territory. He served as corps officer in Caernarvon and Holyhead, Wales and Birmingham, England.

Izzard has contributed several poems to *Assurance* magazine and to *The Officer*. His lyrics to "Dear Lord, I Lift My Heart to Thee" are included in The Salvation Army *Song Book*.

During his tenure at International Headquarters as secretary to the UK territorial commander, Izzard first met Catherine Baird, who was serving as literary secretary. Their mutual respect and friendship served as the inspiration for this book.

John Izzard retired in June 1989 after 42 years of service as a Salvation Army officer. He lives in Birmingham, England and is a soldier of the Birmingham Erdington corps.

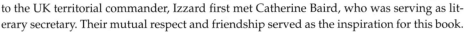

Colonel Henry Gariepy retired as a Salvation Army officer in July 1995, having served the last 15 years as national editor in chief and literary secretary. He has authored 19 books, including *Portraits of Christ*, *Portraits of Perseverance*, the authorized biography of General Eva Burrows and Volume 8 of the International History of The Salvation Army.

Colonel Gariepy's "active retirement" includes speaking engagements, teaching theology at the Army's School for Officer's Training in Suffern, New York and serving as a literary consultant. He and his wife Marjorie live in Toms River, New Jersey.

CREST BOOKS
Salvation Army National Publications

Crest Books, a division of The Salvation Army's National Publications department, was established in 1997 to produce books with a solid biblical foundation and a compelling message on holiness, in keeping with the Army's roots in the Wesleyan tradition.

Never the Same Again
by Shaw Clifton
ISBN: 0-9657601-0-3

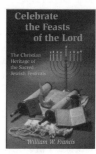

Christians are sometimes overwhelmed by what they feel are confusing explanations of the deeper aspects of faith. The author makes these readily understandable by drawing on his thorough knowledge of Scripture to help seekers establish a sure foundation. Clifton encourages new believers' enthusiasm for Christ while guiding them through roadblocks that can stunt spiritual growth. He addresses such questions as: Can I be sure I'm saved? How much like Jesus can I be? Will God equip me to serve Him? Can I rely on God? This is an ideal resource for new converts, individuals making recommitments, seekers looking to know more about the Christian faith and leaders of discipling groups.

Celebrate the Feasts of the Lord
by William W. Francis
ISBN: 0-9657601-2-X

Author William Francis presents an examination of the feasts and fasts established by God in Leviticus 23, as well as those inaugurated after the Babylonian exile. With studied skill, he examines the historical background of each feast and makes clear its significance for the modern Christian. This book meets a critical need by revealing how Jesus participated in the feasts during His earthly life and how, in Himself, their meaning was fulfilled. Study guides follow each chapter, allowing readers to explore and apply the new insights, and making this book ideal for group study.

Christmas Through the Years:
A War Cry Treasury
ISBN: 0-9657601-1-1

Through the years, the pages of the Christmas *War Cry* have proclaimed the timeless message of the birth of the Babe of Bethlehem. *Christmas Through the Years* contains articles, stories, poetry and art that have inspired readers over the past half century. This treasury highlights Salvationists of wide appeal from General Evangeline Booth (1948) to today's eloquent international leader, John Gowans, and also features contributors such as Billy Graham and Joni Eareckson Tada.

Easter Through the Years:
A War Cry Treasury
ISBN: 0-9657601-7-0

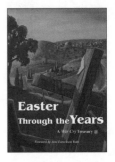

A companion volume to *Christmas Through the Years*, this treasury of work culled from the Easter *War Cry* over the last 50 years recounts the passion of Christ and unpacks the events surrounding the cross and the numerous ways Easter intersects with life and faith today. Contributors include Joni Eareckson Tada, Max Lucado, Commissioner Samuel Logan Brengle and General William Booth.

Fractured Parables
by A. Kenneth Wilson
ISBN: 0-9704870-1-0

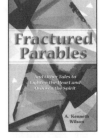

At times it is both fun and beneficial to apply the truths of Scripture to contemporary situations. The people of the Bible are as real as we are today. Wilson helps readers to view beloved biblical accounts in a new light by recasting Jesus' parables in contemporary circumstances and language. His knack for finding humor in the mundane and gems of truth in earthly guise will lighten hearts and quicken spirits.

Pictures from the Word
by Marlene Chase
ISBN: 0-9657601-3-8

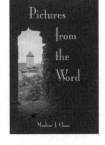

"The Bible is full of beautiful word pictures, concrete images that bring to life spiritual ideas," writes Chase. For instance, "God's personality is poignantly revealed to us in such images as a hen sheltering her chicks or a loving father engraving the names of His children into His hands. These and a host of other images teach us about God and about ourselves." In 56 meditations, the author brings to life the vivid metaphors of Scripture, illuminating familiar passages and addressing the frequent references to the vulnerability of man met by God's limitless and gracious provision.

A Little Greatness
by Joe Noland
ISBN: 0-9657601-4-6

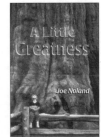

Under the expert tutelage of author Joe Noland, readers explore the book of Acts, revealing the paradoxes of the life of a believer. We can know "common wonders," practice "defiant obedience," be "lowered to new heights" and assert "gentle boldness." Using word play and alliteration, Noland draws the reader into the story of the early Church and reveals the contemporary relevance of all that took place. The book is divided into three parts, which address shared aspects of heavenly greatness available through the help of the Holy Spirit: great power, great grace and great joy. A Bible study and discussion guide for each chapter helps the reader apply each lesson, making this an ideal group study resource.

Romance & Dynamite: Essays on Science and the Nature of Faith
by Lyell M. Rader
ISBN: 0-9657601-5-4

"Whatever God makes works, and works to perfection. So does His plan for turning life from a rat race to a rapture." This and other anecdotes and insights on the interplay of science and faith are found in this collection of essays by one of the Army's most indefatigable evangelists. As a Salvation Army officer, the author used his training as a chemist to prove the trustworthiness of the Bible, find evidence of the Creator's hand in everything and demonstrate why the saving knowledge of God is crucial to understanding life's value and purpose.

Who Are These Salvationists?
by Shaw Clifton
ISBN: 0-9657601-6-2

Clifton has written a seminal study that explores the Army's roots, theology and position in the body of believers and provides readers with a definitive profile of Salvationism and Salvationists. This study helps Salvationists to understand their historical and theological roots and shape their understanding of the Army's mission in the new century. The book also provides non–Salvationists with the most comprehensive portrait of the Army and its soldiers produced to date and introduces them to the theology which drives our social action.

Slightly Off Center! Growth Principles to Thaw Frozen Paradigms
by Terry Camsey
ISBN: 0-9657601-8-9

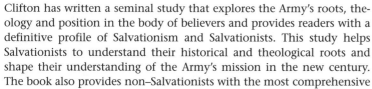

As an expert in the field of church health, Camsey seeks to thaw frozen paradigms of what is "Army." He challenges us to see things from a different perspective, thus throwing our perspectives slightly off center. Camsey urges us to welcome a new generation of Salvationists whose methods may be different, but whose hearts are wholly God's and whose mission remains consistent with the fundamental principles William Booth established.

He Who Laughed First: Delighting in a Holy God
by Phil Needham
ISBN: 0-8341-1872-6

In this first joint–venture publishing project undertaken by Crest Books and Beacon Hill Press, Needham questions why there are so many sour–faced saints when the Christian life is meant to be joyful. In his book he explores the secret to enduring joy, a joy that is not found by following some list of prescriptions, but by letting God make us holy, by letting Him free us to become who we are in Christ: saints. *He Who Laughed First* helps the reader discover the why and how of becoming a joyful, hilarious saint.

A Salvationist Treasury
edited by Henry Gariepy
ISBN: 0-9657601-9-7

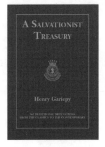

This book brings to readers the quintessence of devotional writings from Salvationist authors spanning over 100 years. From Army notables to the virtually unknown, from the classics to the contemporary, this treasure trove of 365 inspirational readings will enrich your life, deepen your devotional study and enhance your grasp of the Army's principles and mission. *A Salvationist Treasury* is certain to become a milestone compilation of Army literature.

Our God Comes: And Will Not Be Silent
by Marlene Chase
ISBN: 0-9704870-0-2

Our God Comes rests on the premise that, like the unstoppable ocean tide, God comes to us in a variety of ways and His voice will not be silent as He reveals Himself throughout all Creation. This book of poetry, the first of its kind for Crest Books, invites the reader to contemplate life's experiences and God's goodness to us. An accomplished writer and poet, Chase offers a book that lends itself to devotional meditation, small group discussion and the literary enjoyment of carefully crafted poetry.

If Two Shall Agree
by Carroll Ferguson Hunt
ISBN: 083-411-9285

In this second collaboration with Beacon Hill Press, Crest Books shares the fascinating story of how God brought Paul and Kay Rader together and melded them into a team who served in The Salvation Army for over 35 years. Readers will follow on the journey from General Rader's memories of his parents' innovative ministry in New York to his election to the highest office in the Army and then as president of Asbury College. Combined with the vision of his wife, Kay, for greater ministry of women in the Army, one can see the power and far-reaching influence in a couple serving together as one in the name of Christ.

For order information, contact the Supplies and Purchasing department nearest you:

Atlanta, GA—(800) 786-7372
Des Plaines, IL—(847) 294-2012
Rancho Palos Verdes, CA—(800) 937-8896
West Nyack, NY—(888) 488-4882